REVISE KEY STAGE 2 SATs
Mathematics

TEN-MINUTE TESTS

Series Consultant: Harry Smith
Author: Giles Clare

Also available to support revision:

Revise Key Stage 2 SATs English Ten-Minute Tests: 9781292216669

Revision is more than just these tests:

Other KS2 SATs Mathematics titles in the Revise series include:

For the full range of Pearson revision titles visit:
www.pearsonschools.co.uk/revise

Contents

Tests

Set A
1	Test 1
3	Test 2
5	Test 3
7	Test 4
10	Test 5
13	Test 6
16	Test 7
19	Test 8
22	Test 9
25	Test 10
28	Test 11
31	Scoresheet

Set B
32	Test 1
34	Test 2
37	Test 3
39	Test 4
41	Test 5
43	Test 6
46	Test 7
49	Test 8
52	Test 9
55	Test 10
58	Test 11
61	Scoresheet

Answers

Set A
62   Tests 1–11

Set B
70   Tests 1–11

Before you start

You have 10 minutes to complete each test. Each test is worth 10 marks.
For some questions, you may get a mark for showing your method.
Make sure you have:
- a pen, a pencil and a rubber
- a ruler and a protractor
- a mirror.

You are not allowed to use a calculator or tracing paper.
The number under each line at the side of the page tells you the maximum number of marks for each question.

We have tried to make the Ten-Minute Tests match the real tests as closely as possible. The number of marks you need to earn per minute is the same as in a full set of real tests.

A small bit of small print
The Standards and Testing Agency publishes Sample Test Materials on its website. This is the official content and this book should be used in conjunction with it. The questions in this book have been written to help you practise what you have learned in your revision. Remember: the real test questions may not look like this.

Set A Test 1

1 Eight people sprinted as far as they could.

Racers	Sophie	Eden	Kush	Hollie	Jared	Mike	Naomi	Owen
Distance (to nearest 10 m)	120	90	140	70	80	130	60	150

What is the **mean** distance sprinted by the racers?

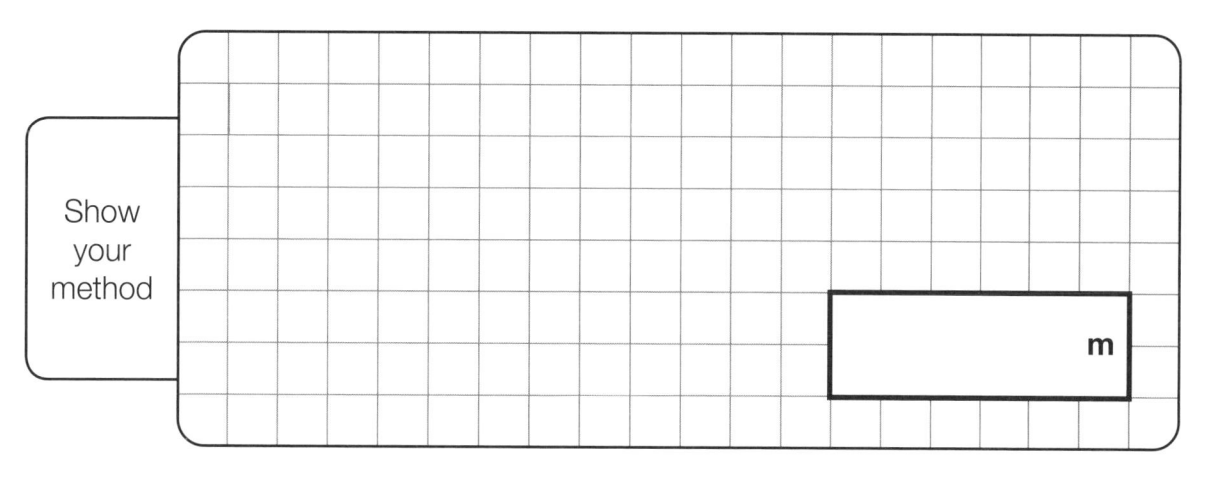

Show your method

m

2 marks

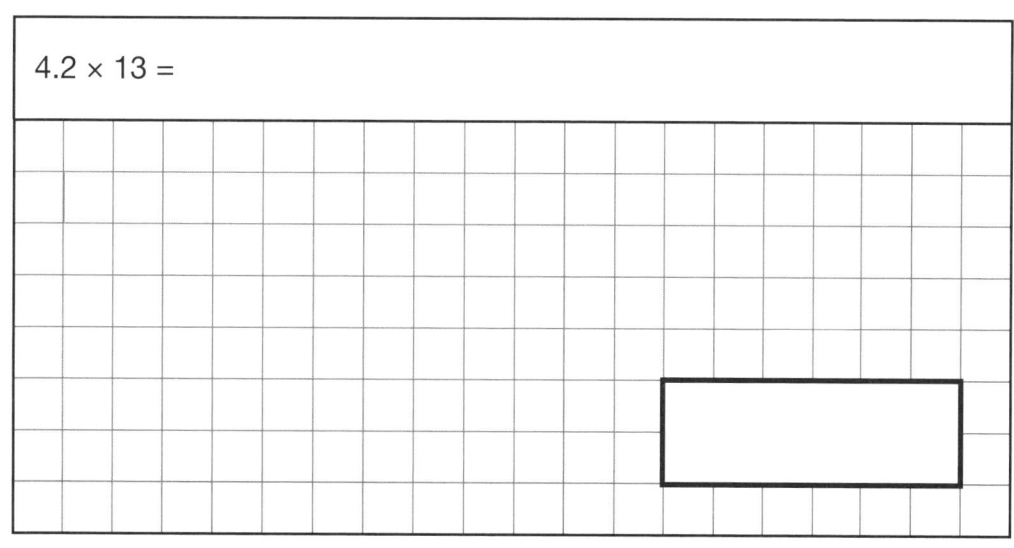

2 4.2 × 13 =

1 mark

3 55% of 300 =

1 mark

Set A Test 1

4 Amelia chooses a number less than 50
She multiplies it by 4 and then subtracts 8
She then divides the answer by 8
Her answer is 7.5

What was the number she started with?

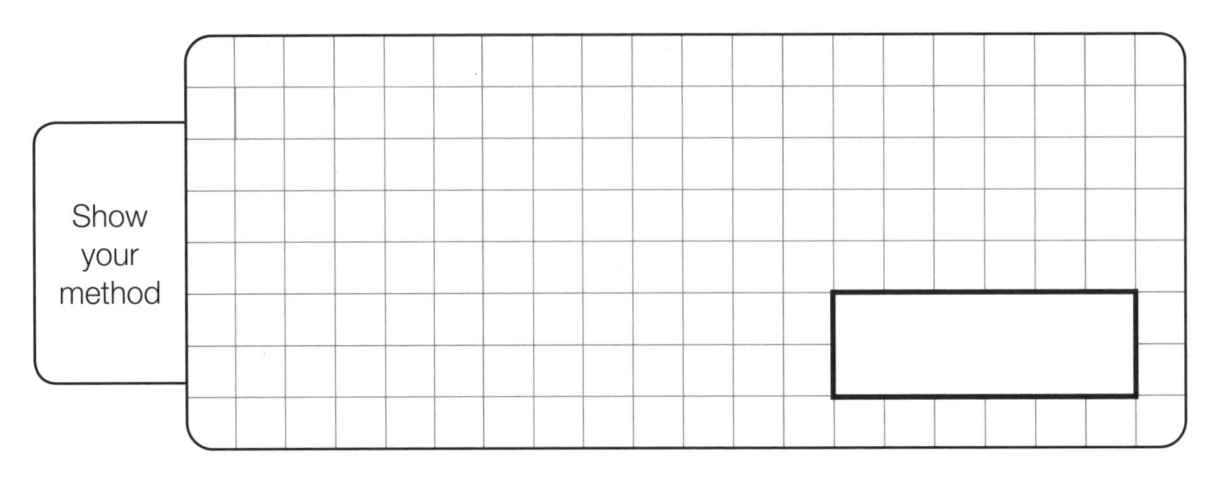

Show your method

2 marks

5 Last week, Tamwar filled his swimming pool $\frac{3}{5}$ full.
This morning, he added another 50,000 litres to fill the pool completely.

How many litres of water does Tamwar's pool hold when it is **full**?

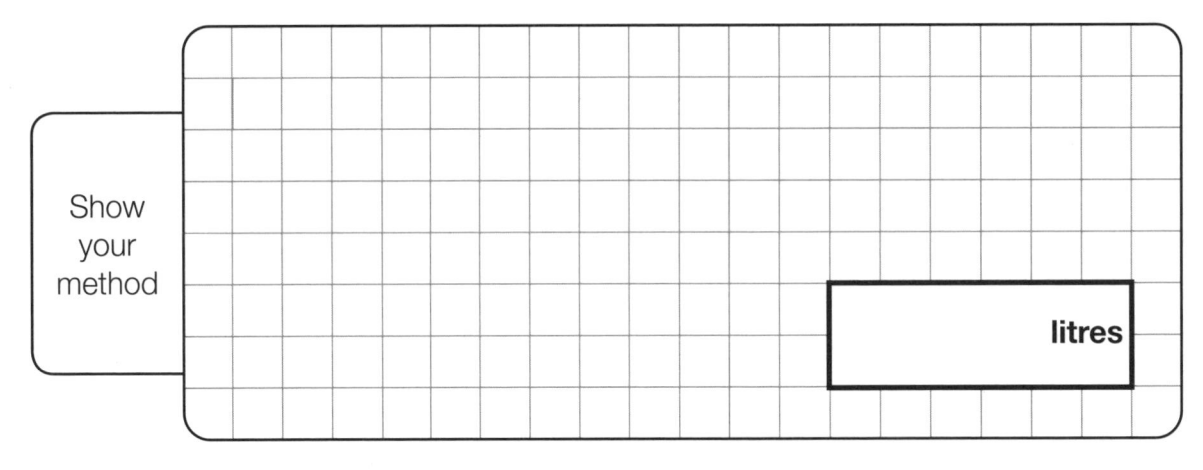

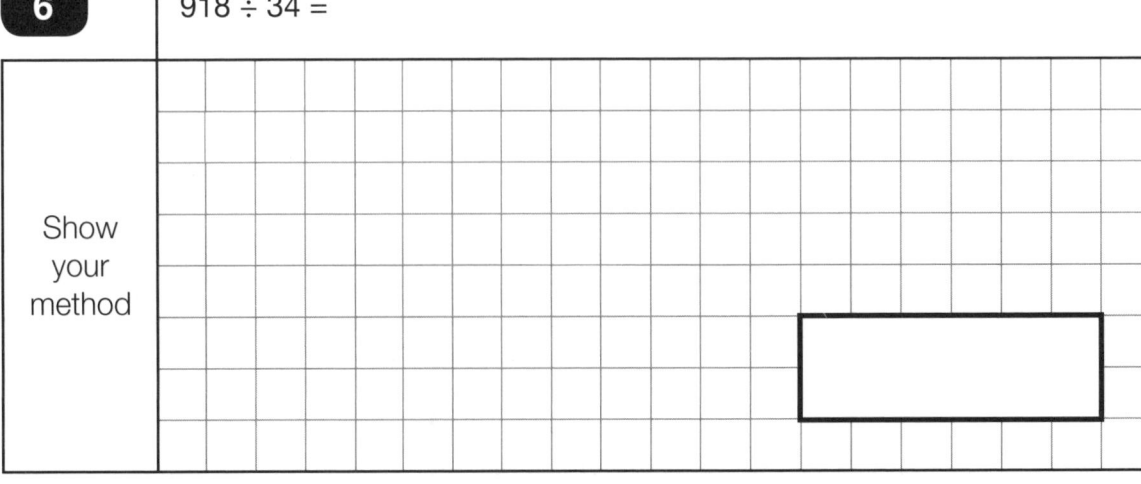

Show your method

litres

2 marks

6 $918 \div 34 =$

Show your method

2 marks

[END OF TEST]

Set A Test 2

1 Write in the missing numbers.

Number	Rounded to the nearest whole number
3.55	
5.05	

Number	Rounded to the nearest tenth
1.14	
0.95	

2 marks

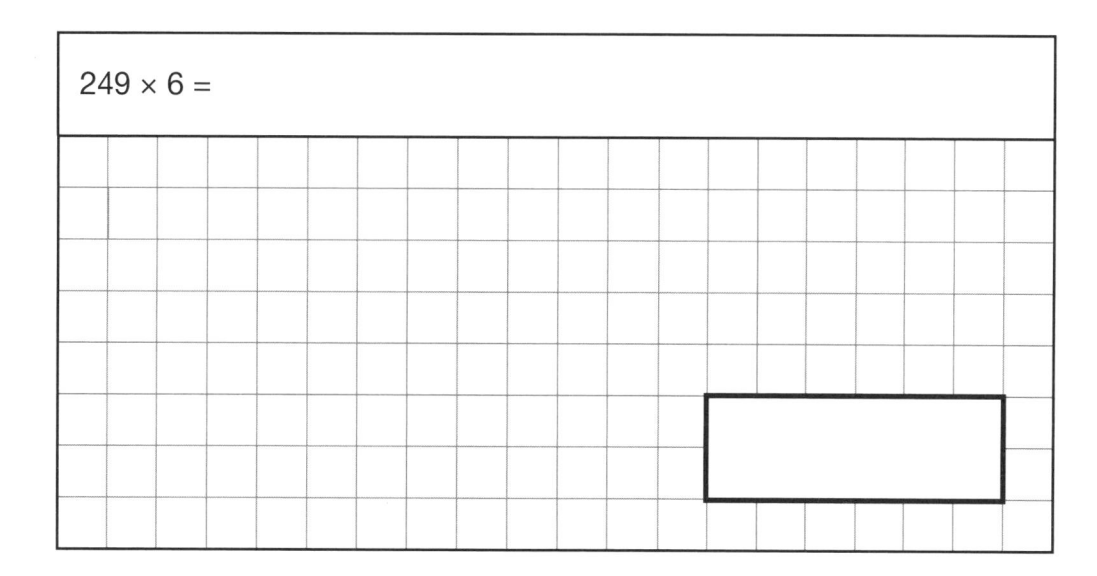

2 249 × 6 =

1 mark

3 Kamal and Lola each have a suitcase.

Kamal's suitcase weighs $15\frac{1}{4}$ kg. Lola's suitcase weighs 15.47 kg.

How much more does Lola's suitcase weigh than Kamal's?

Give your answer in grams.

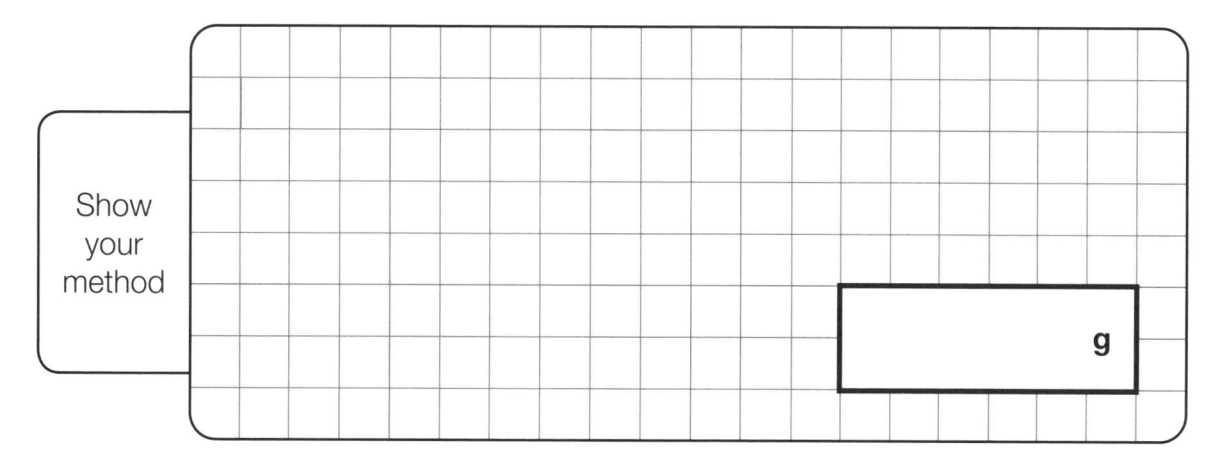

Show your method

g

2 marks

Set A Test 2

4 3,094 ÷ 14 =

Show your method

2 marks

5 The shaded shape is translated from A to B and reduced in size by a scale factor of 2

Draw the reduced shape on the grid.

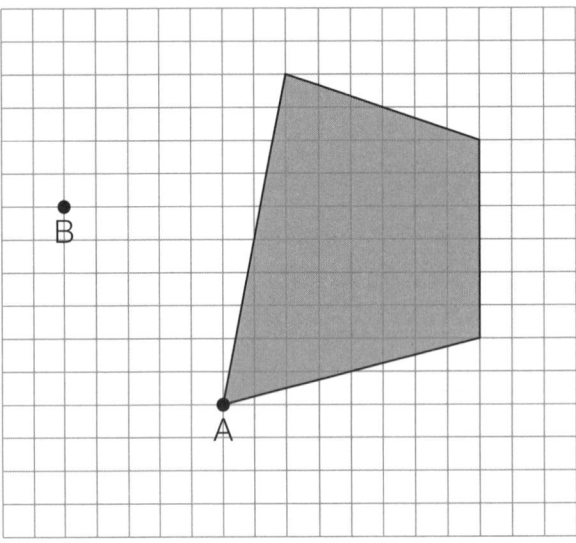

2 marks

6 100 × 680 =

1 mark

[END OF TEST]

1 928 + 100 =

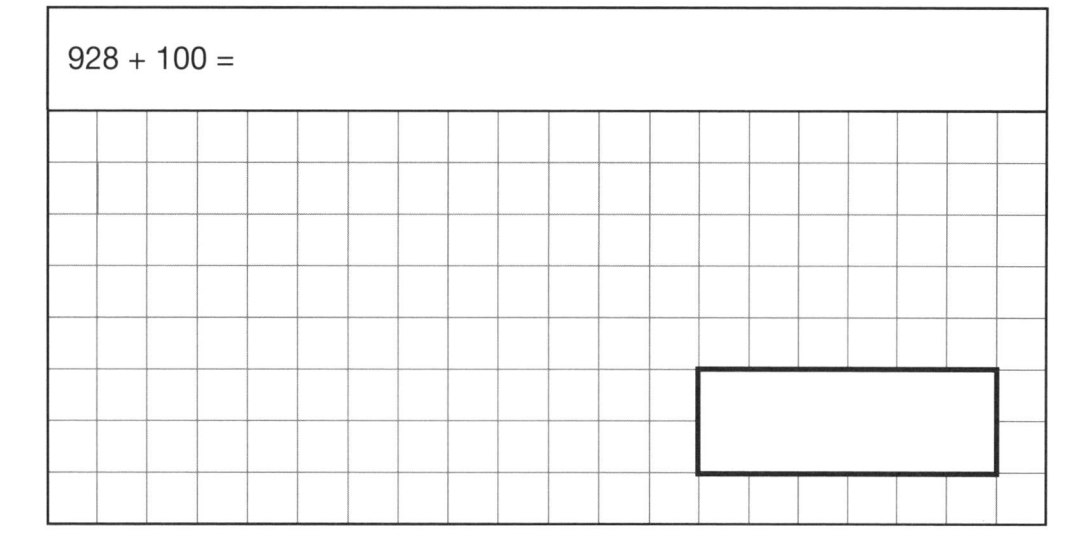

　　　　　　　　　　　　　　　　　　　　　　　1 mark

2 A race track is 4 km long. The race lasts 10 laps.

There are 5 miles in 8 km. How far is the race in miles?

　　　　　　　　　　　　　　　　　miles

　　　　　　　　　　　　　　　　　　　　　　　1 mark

3 Write these numbers in order, starting with the **smallest**.

2^3　　4^2　　1^3　　2^2　　3^2

smallest

　　　　　　　　　　　　　　　　　　　　　　　1 mark

4 13 × 8.3 =

　　　　　　　　　　　　　　　　　　　　　　　1 mark

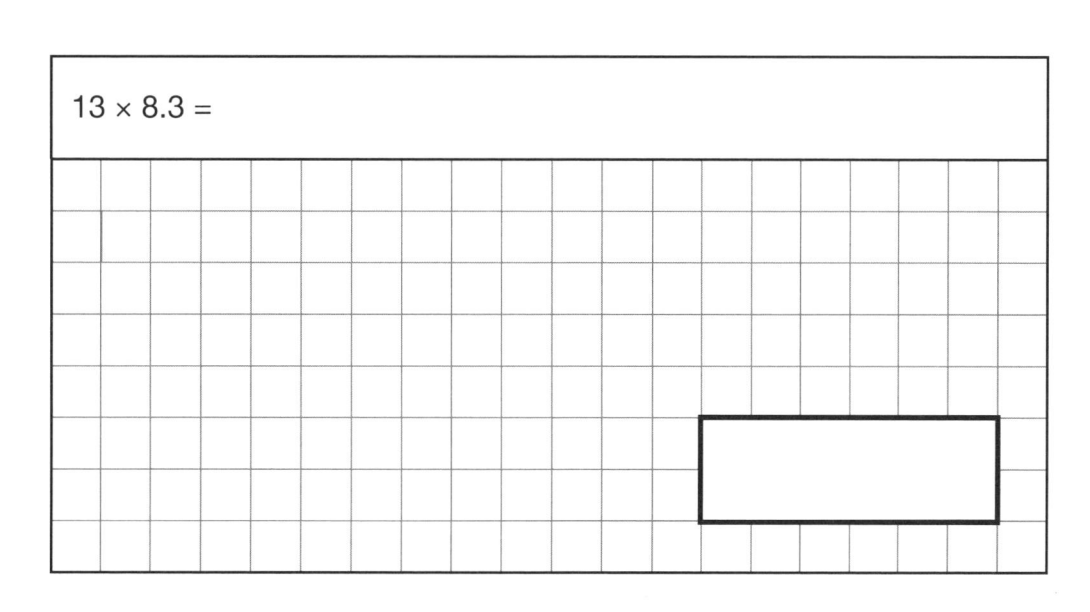

Set A Test 3

Set A Test 3

5 Freddie is saving up for a video game. He has £39.60
The game costs £44.99

How much **more** money does Freddie need to save?

1 mark

6 $3x + y = 25$

What is x when $y = 10$?

1 mark

7 $593 \times 41 =$

Show your method

2 marks

8 Lara spends $\frac{3}{5}$ of her holiday money on the hotel. She has £302 left.

How much money did she start with?

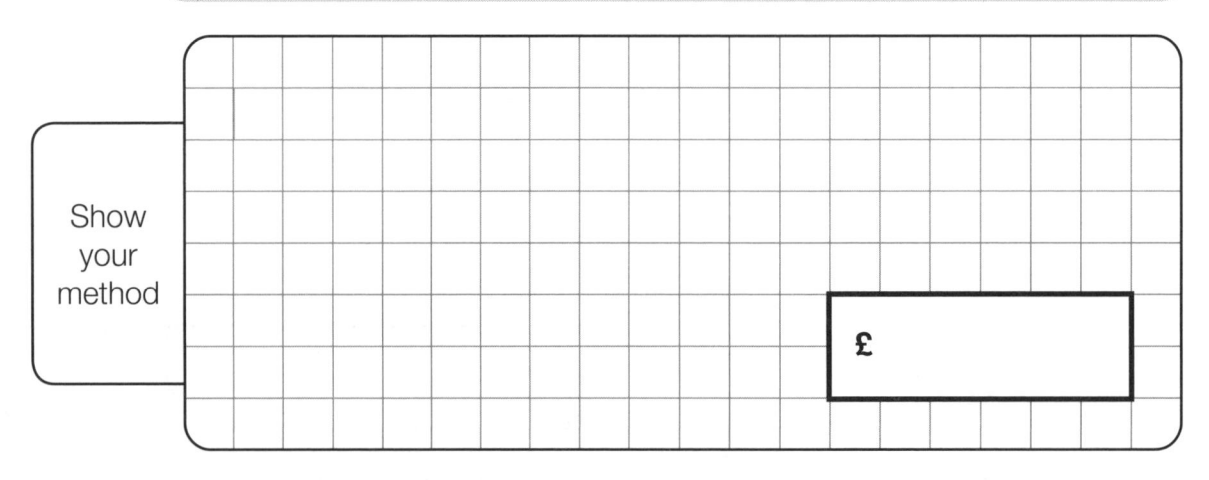

Show your method

£

2 marks

[END OF TEST]

1 48 + 212 =

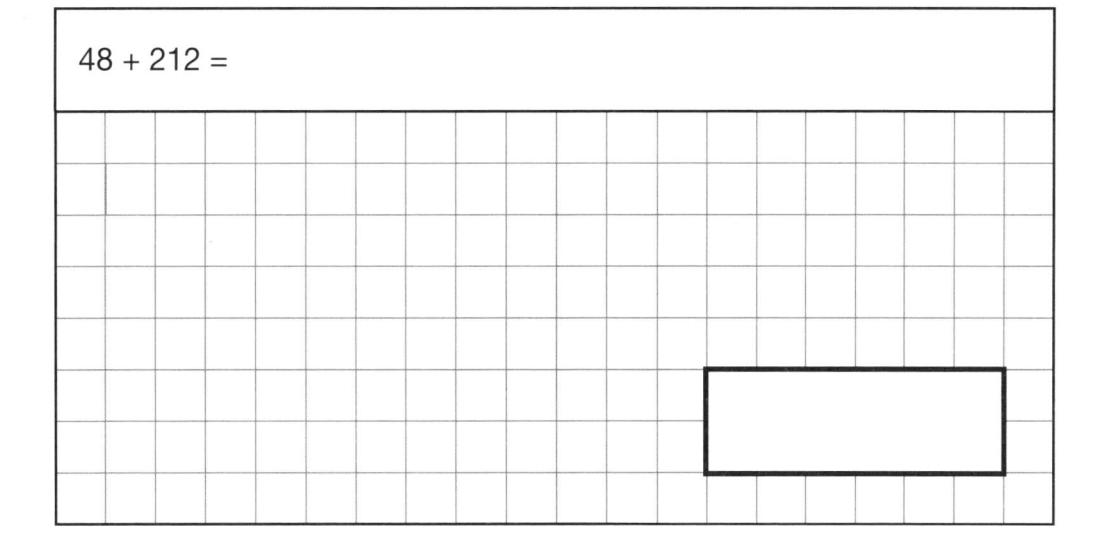

1 mark

2 Round **596,315**

to the nearest 1,000

to the nearest 100,000

1 mark

3 What is 65 days in weeks and days?

weeks   days

1 mark

Set A Test 4

4 A shaded **scalene** triangle is drawn inside this square.

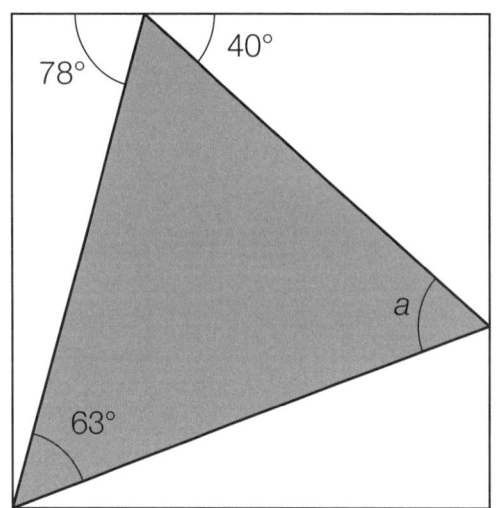

Not to scale

Calculate the size of angle *a*.

Show your method

a is _____ °

2 marks

5 547 − 8 =

1 mark

6 Write the four missing digits to make this **addition** correct.

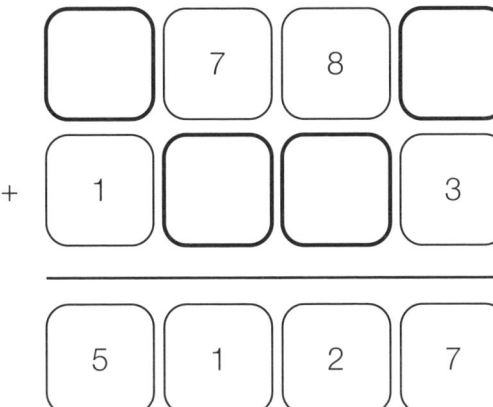

2 marks

7 60 × 40 =

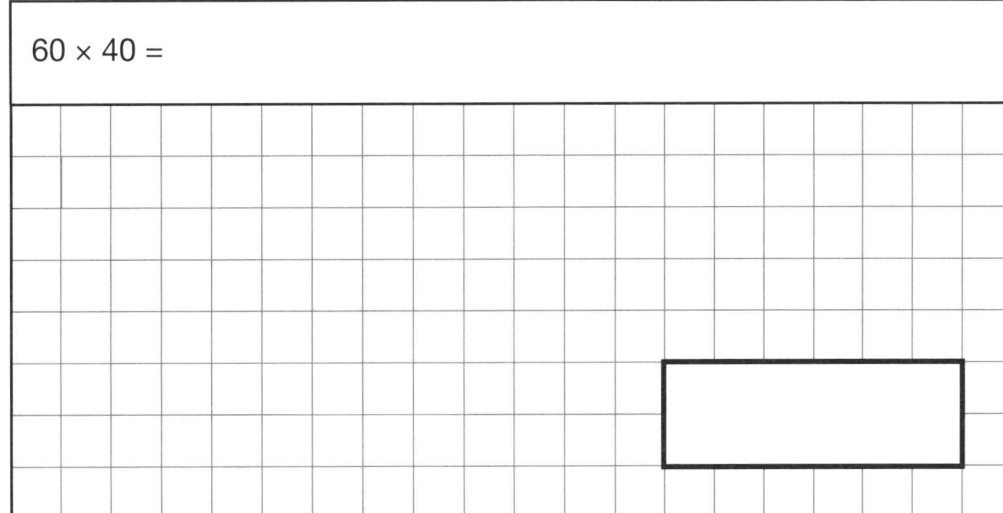

1 mark

8 What number is halfway between 10.3 and 11.0?

1 mark

[END OF TEST]

Set A Test 5

1. 72 ÷ 3 =

_____
1 mark

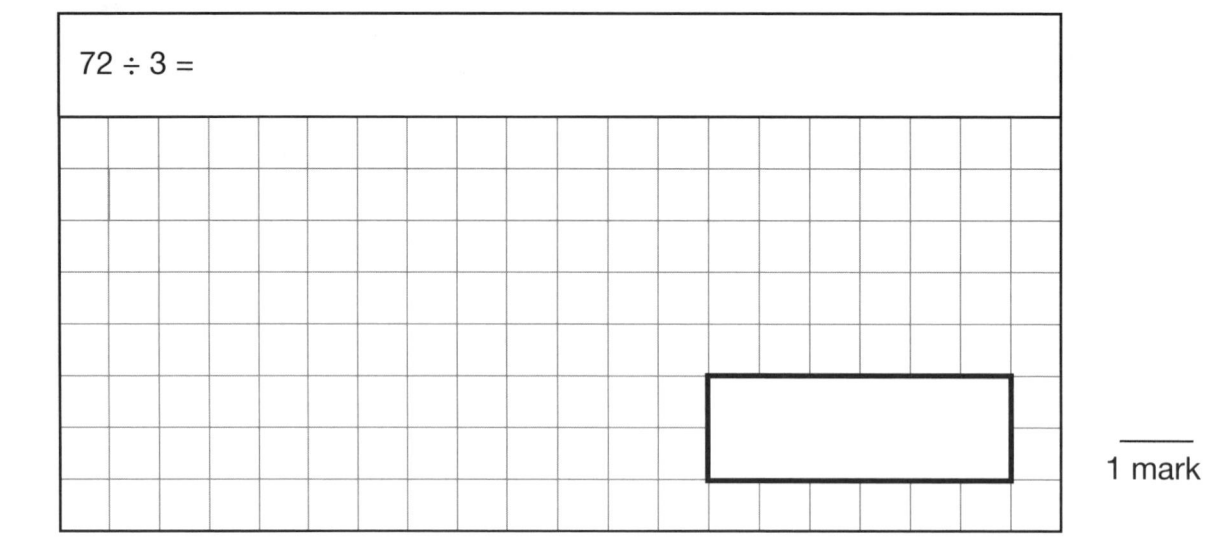

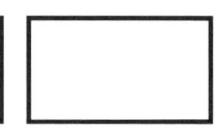

2. Write these numbers in order, starting with the **smallest**.

11.092   10.039   12.03   11.1   11.03

smallest

_____
1 mark

3. $\frac{6}{9} + \frac{7}{9} =$

_____
1 mark

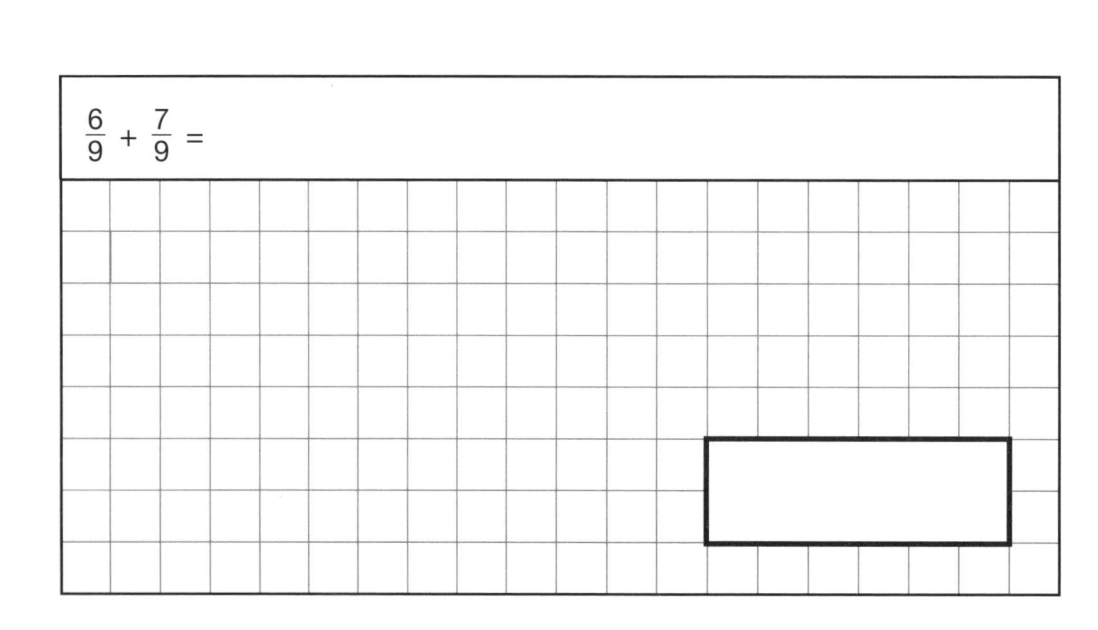

4 This 3D shape is called an icosahedron. Some of its faces are shaded.

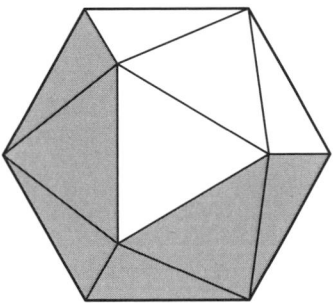

Here is the net for the same shape.

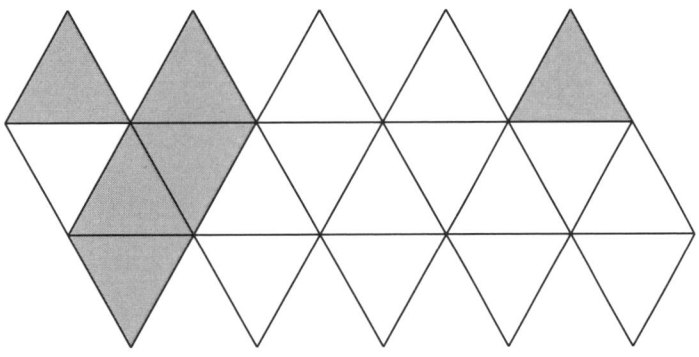

What percentage of the faces of the icosahedron is shaded?

[ ] %

1 mark

5 81 × 37 =

Show your method

2 marks

Set A Test 5

6 Here are two triangles on coordinate axes.

The shaded triangle is the same shape as the unshaded one but it has been enlarged by a scale factor of 2

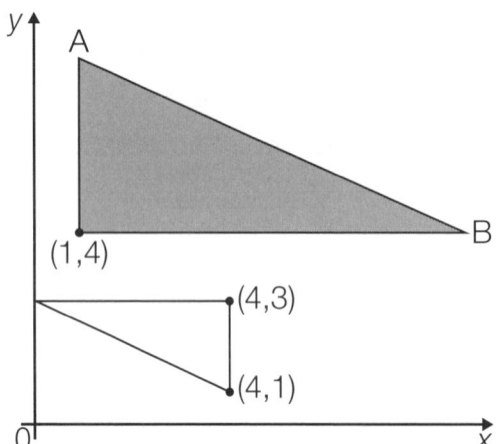

Not to scale

Write the coordinates of points **A** and **B**.

A = (,)

B = (,)

2 marks

7 Here is a diagram for sorting numbers.

Write **one number** in each box.

One is done for you.

	multiple of 4	**not** a multiple of 4
multiple of 6		18
not a multiple of 6		

2 marks

[END OF TEST]

1 Here is a number written in Roman numerals.

LXIV

Write the number in figures.

1 mark

2 Maisie pours an **extra** 150 millilitres of water into this measuring cylinder.

Draw an arrow on the cylinder to show the new level of the water.

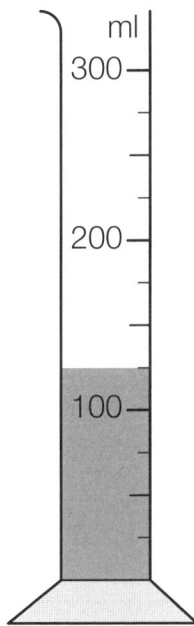

1 mark

3 $\frac{8}{10} \div 4 =$

1 mark

4 Here is a shaded shape on a grid.

The shape is translated so that point **X** moves to point **Y**.

Draw the shape in its new position.

Use a ruler.

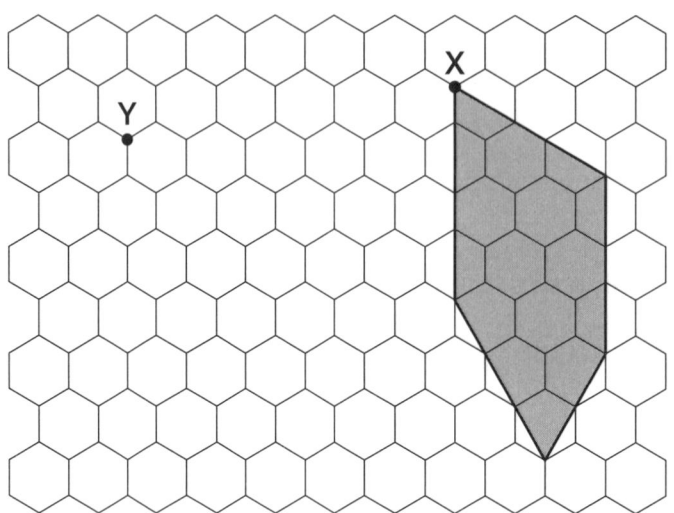

2 marks

5 1.3 ÷ 100 =

1 mark

6 At the cinema, pick and mix sweets cost 75p for 50g.

What is the cost of 300g of sweets?

Give your answer in pounds and pence.

Show your method

£ _____

2 marks

7 Complete these fractions to make each one equivalent to $\frac{3}{4}$

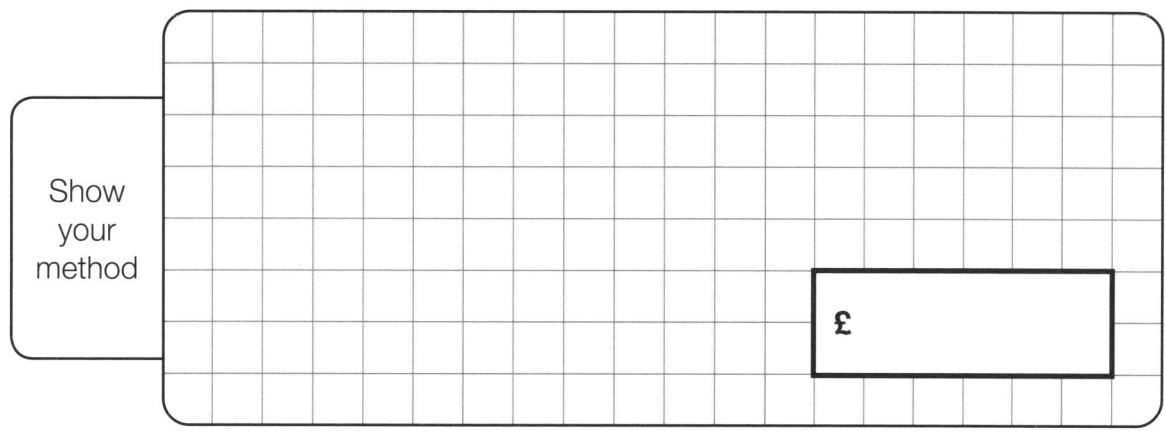

1 mark

8 $25 - 4^2 =$

1 mark

[END OF TEST]

Set A Test 7

1 Put these temperatures in order, starting with the **lowest**.

9°C   −11°C   −23°C   12°C   0°C

lowest

1 mark

2 5,231 × 42 =

Show your method

2 marks

3 $n = 32$

What is $3n - 5$?

1 mark

$4q + 50 = 210$

Work out the value of q.

1 mark

4 Match each decimal number to its equivalent fraction.

One has been done for you.

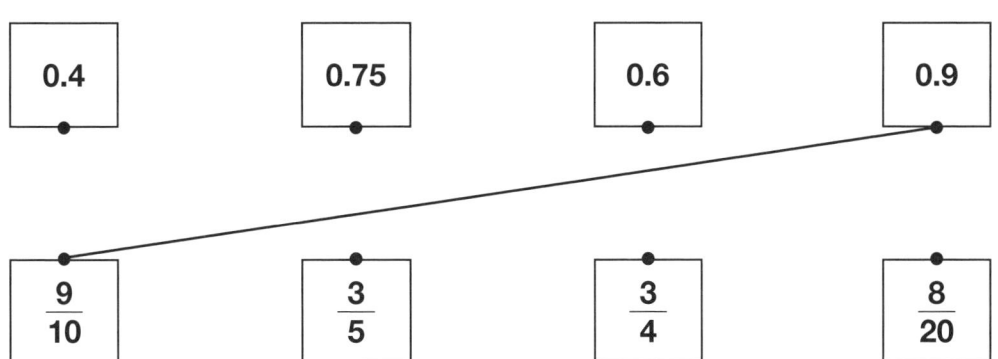

1 mark

5

$\frac{3}{5} \times 120 =$

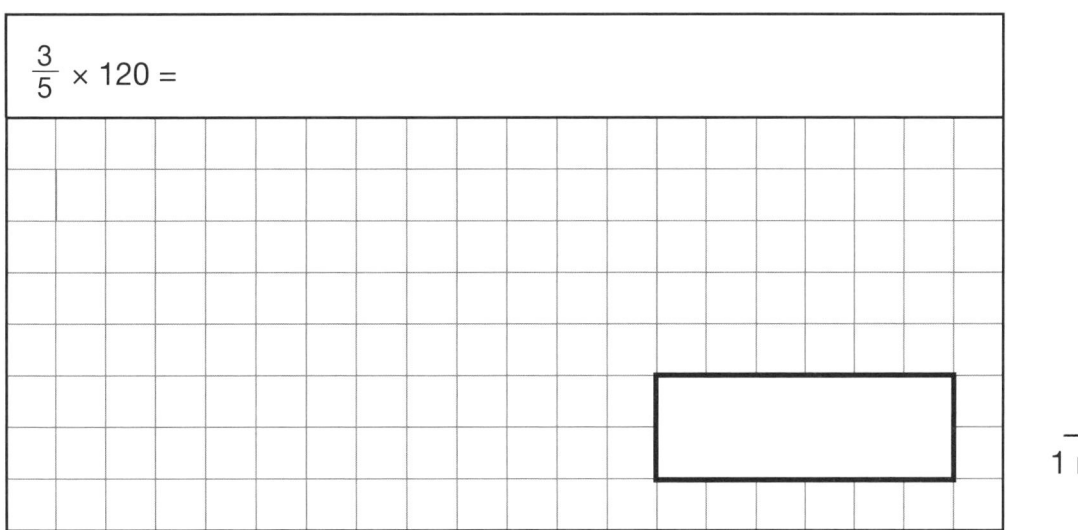

1 mark

6

857 + 475 =

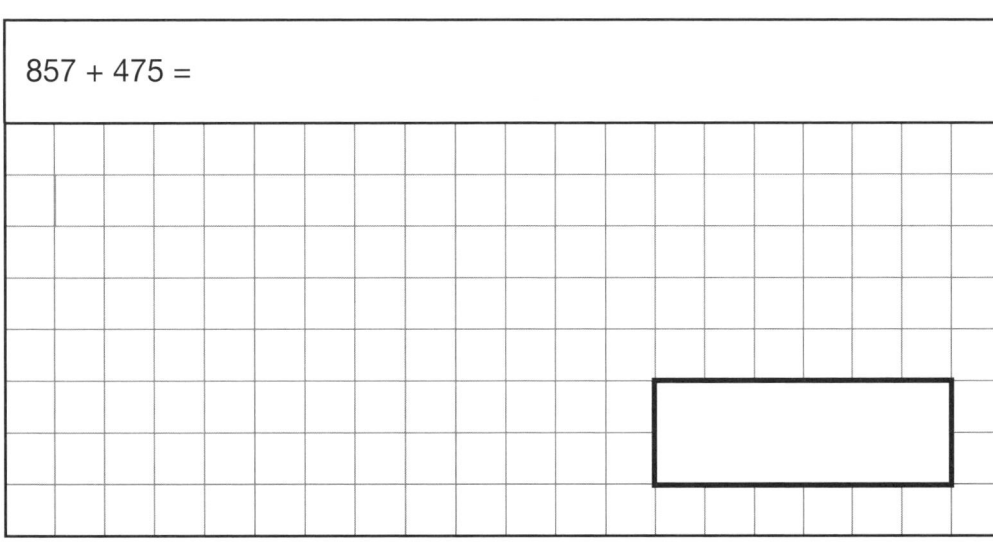

1 mark

7 Look at this 3D shape.

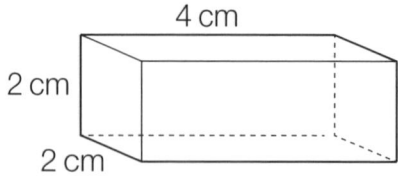

Draw two more faces on this centimetre dotted paper to complete the net of this shape.

Use a ruler.

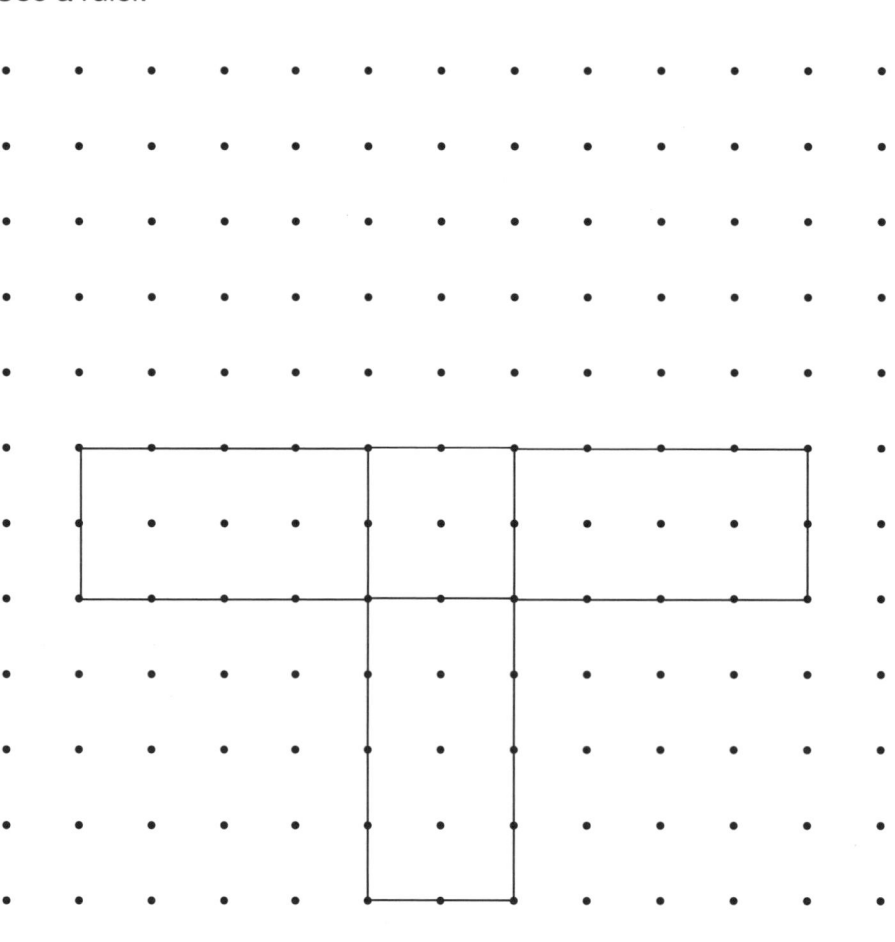

2 marks

[END OF TEST]

Set A Test 8

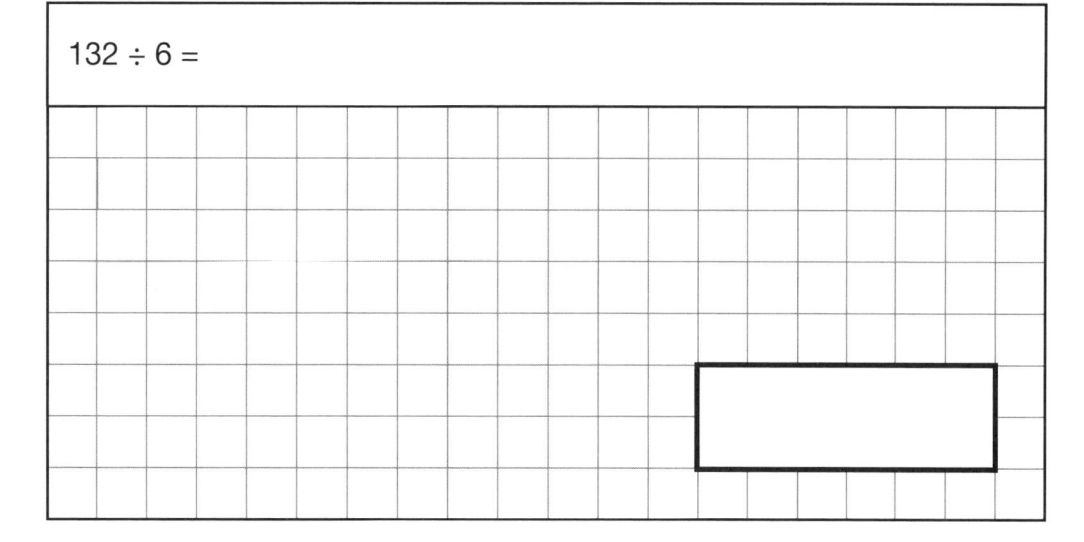

1 132 ÷ 6 =

1 mark

2 Write these fractions in order, starting with the **smallest**.

$\frac{4}{10}$ $\frac{3}{5}$ $\frac{1}{2}$ $\frac{18}{20}$ $\frac{1}{5}$

smallest

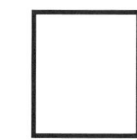

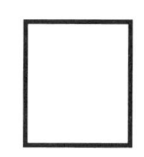

1 mark

3 What **pairs** of whole numbers numbers less than 7 could be hidden under the two counters?

● + 3 = ○

black =   white =

black =   white =

black =   white =

1 mark

4 1,433 + 19,881 =

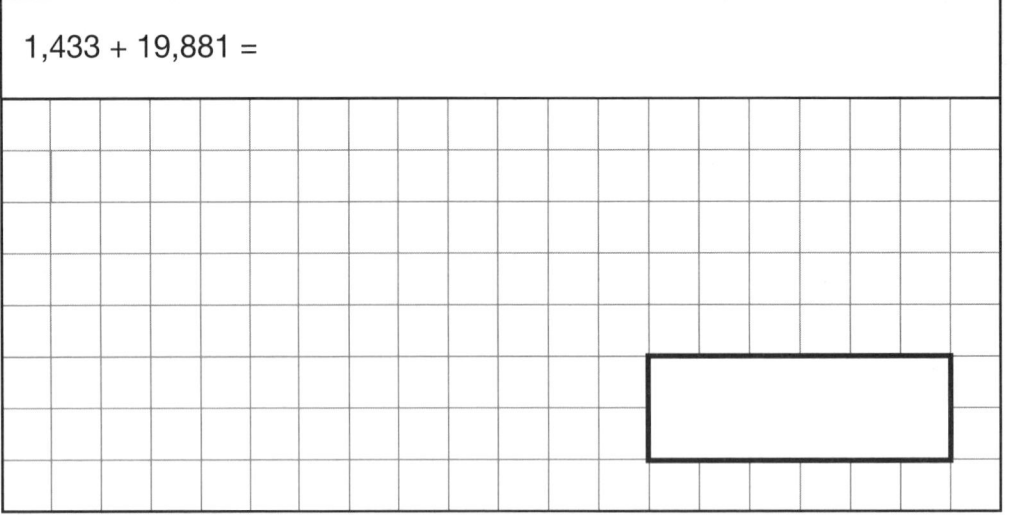

1 mark

5 Callum has some identical rectangles.

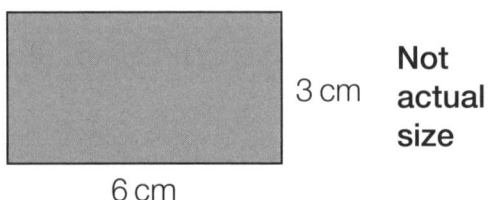

3 cm   Not actual size

6 cm

He uses four of the rectangles to make this shape.

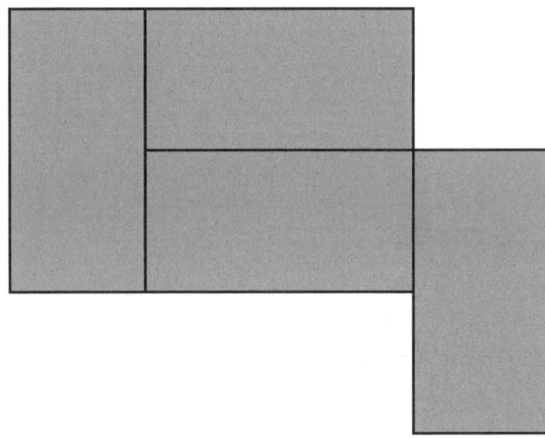

What is the **perimeter** of Callum's new shape?

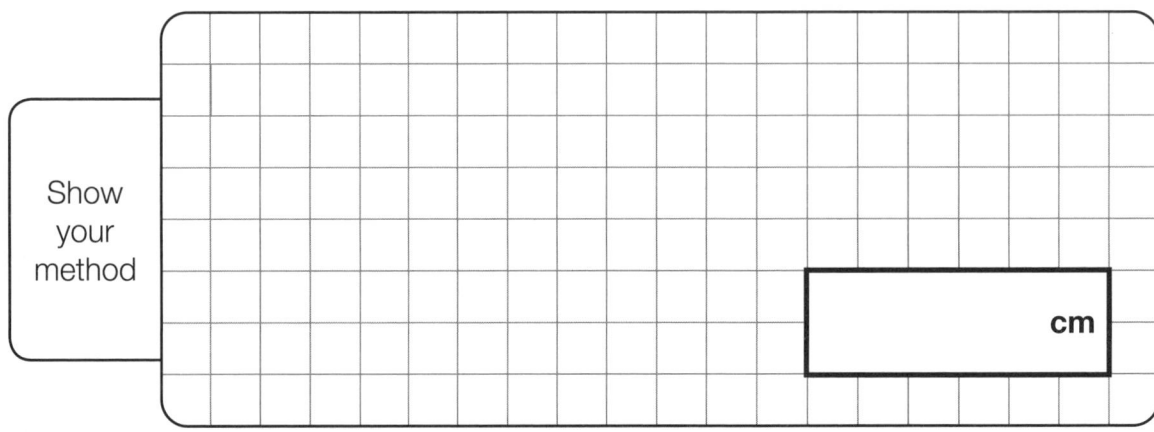

Show your method

cm

2 marks

Set A Test 8

6 Tomas, Maxine and Romesh sold some cupcakes for charity.
They baked 120 cakes altogether.
Tomas sold 25 cakes.
Maxine sold 10 cakes.
Romesh sold twice as many cakes as the others put together.

How many cakes were left at the end?

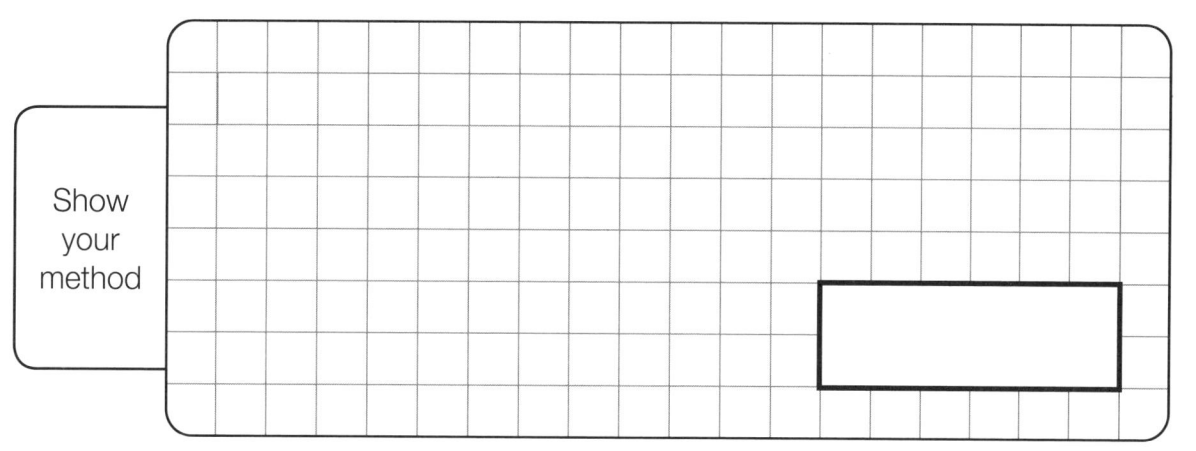

Show your method

2 marks

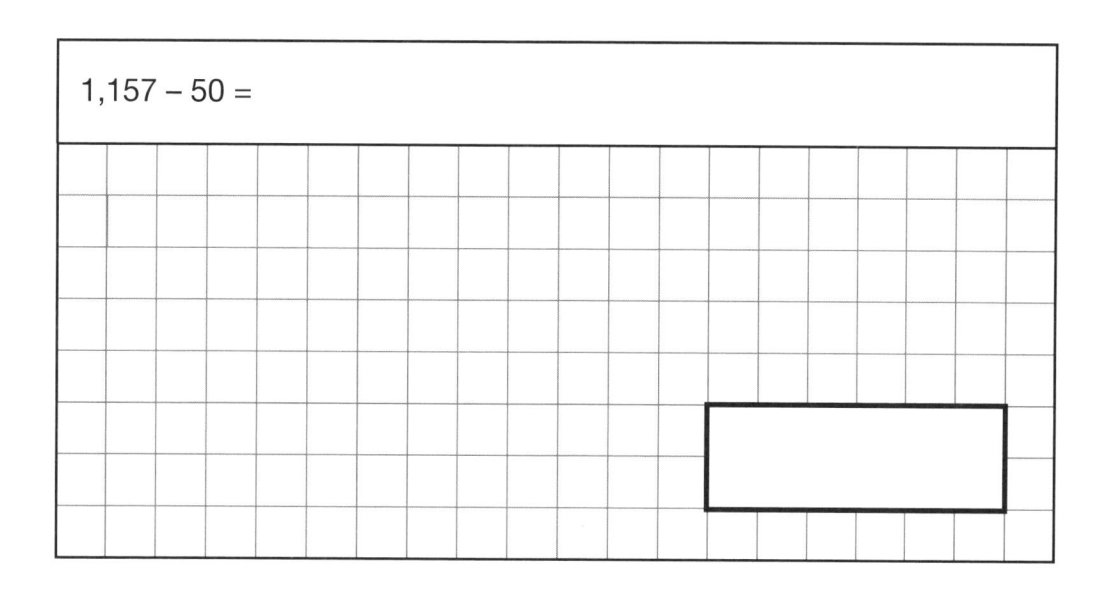

7 1,157 − 50 =

1 mark

8 Two groups of children share 180 biscuits in the ratio 2 : 7

How many biscuits does each group get?

group 1 ☐   group 2 ☐

1 mark

[END OF TEST]

Set A Test 9

1 Subtract 10^3 from 4,081

⬜

1 mark

2 The rule of this sequence of numbers is "add 4 each time".

1   5   9   ...

Adil says,

"Because you are adding an even number, some of the numbers in the sequence will be multiples of 2"

Adil is wrong.

Explain how you know.

1 mark

3 2.98 + 7.018 =

1 mark

4 These circles represent the chain rings on a bicycle.

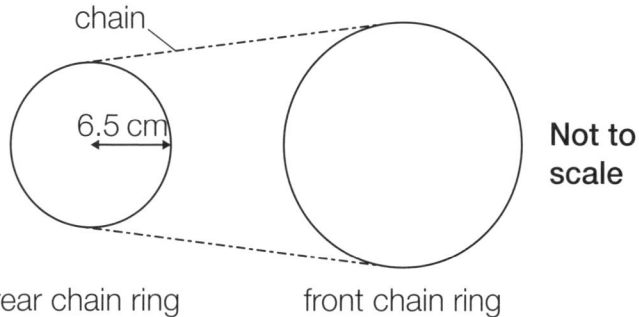

The diameter of the front chain ring is $1\frac{1}{2}$ times the size of the diameter of the rear chain ring.

What is the diameter of the front chain ring?

Show your method

cm

2 marks

5 $4^3 + 6 =$

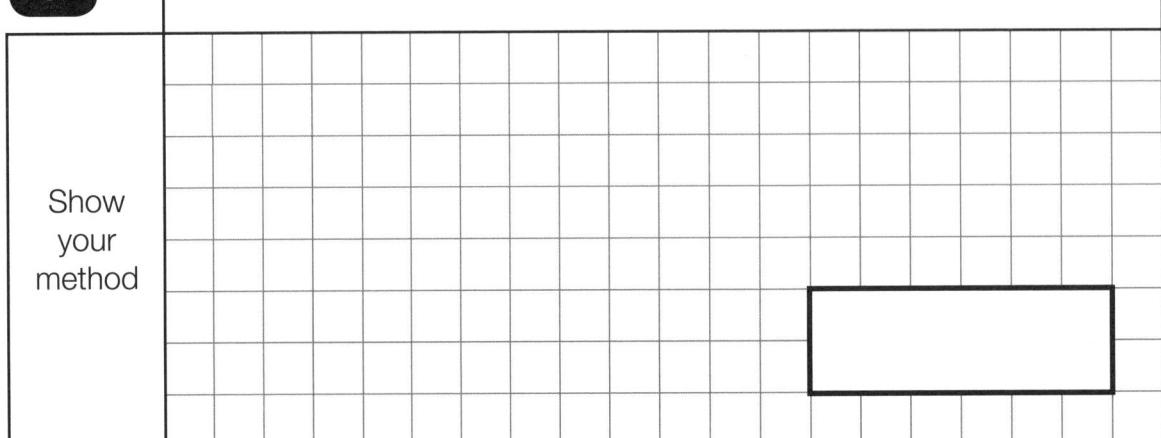

_____
1 mark

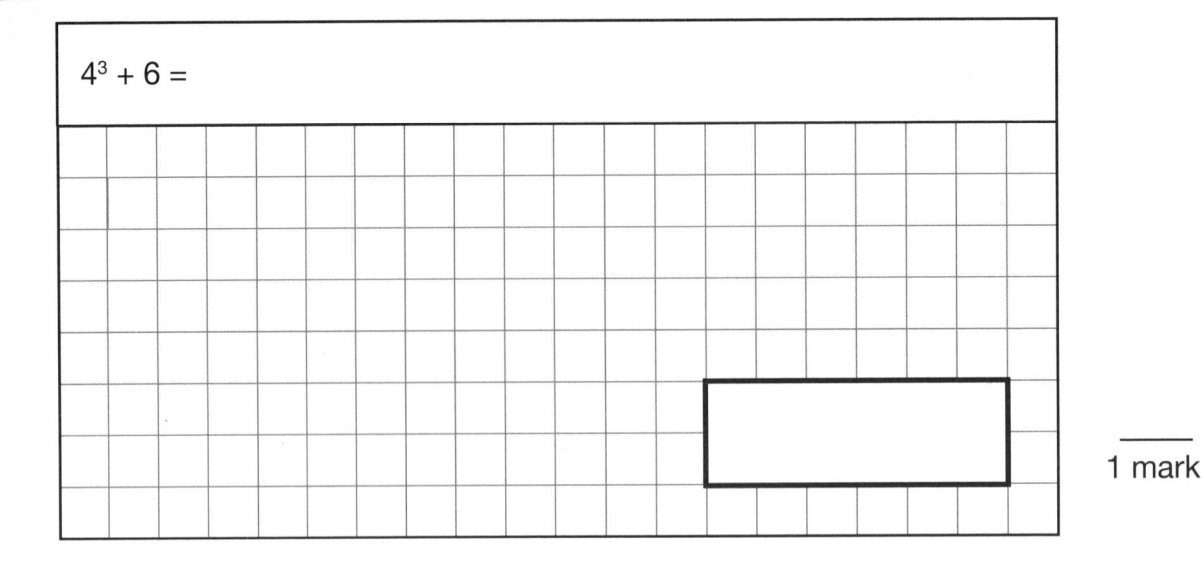

6   In one week, Molly collects £43.50 for charity.

The following week, she raises another £62.05

She then donates the money equally to 5 different charities.

How much money does she give to each charity?

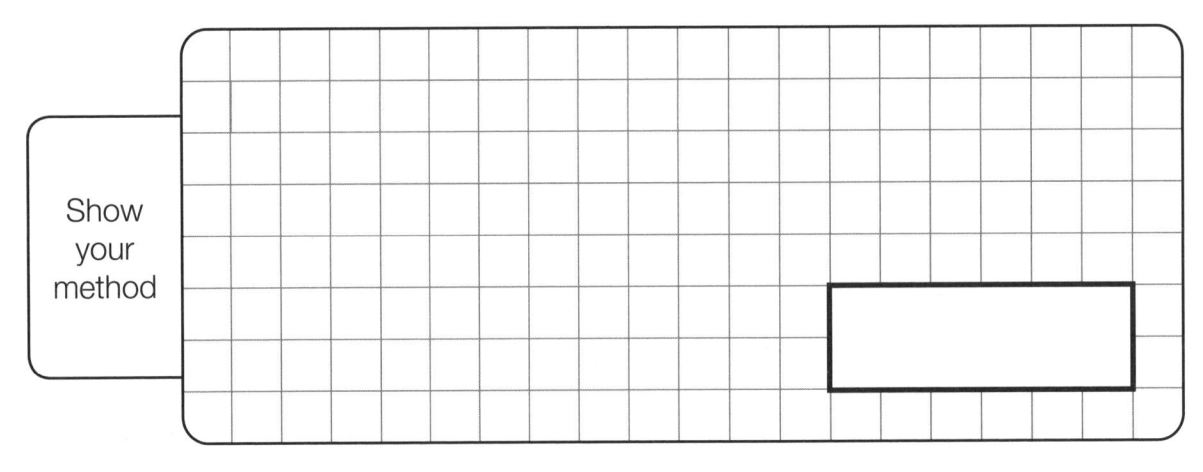

Show your method

_____
2 marks

7 $736 \div 16 =$

Show your method

_____
2 marks

[END OF TEST]

1 410,328 − 8,999 =

1 mark

2 A car manufacturer produces four different models. The pie chart compares the money the company made from the four models last year.

The company made 5 times more money on saloon models than sports models.

The total sales were £120 million.

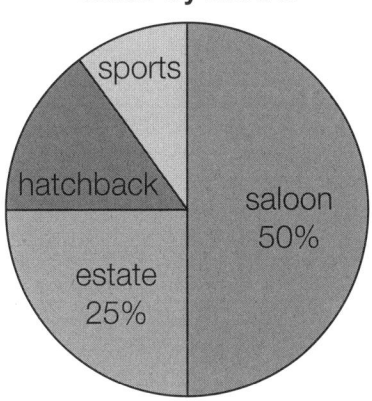

Sales by model

How much money did the company make from hatchbacks last year?

Show your method

£

2 marks

Set A Test 10

3 Sunetra thinks of a number.
She multiplies it by 7 and adds 5
From this, she subtracts her original number.
The answer is 23

> Use algebra to write this missing number problem. Use **n** for the number Sunetra is thinking of.

[   ]

1 mark

> What number is Sunetra thinking of?

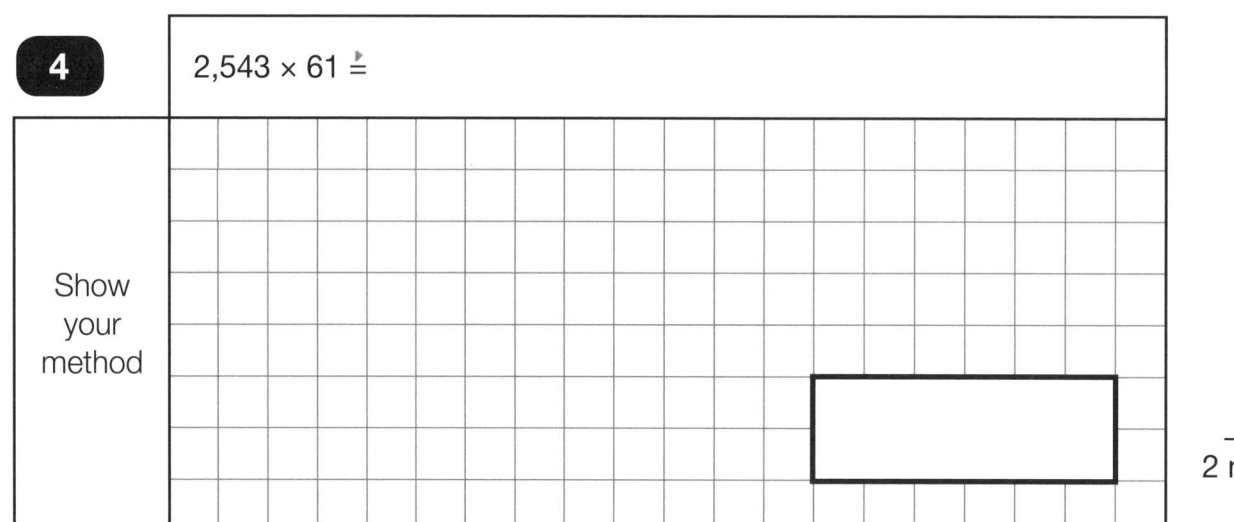

n = [   ]

1 mark

4 2,543 × 61 =

Show your method

2 marks

5 Here is a grid of 20 squares.

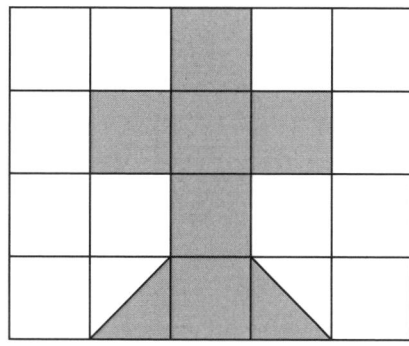

What fraction of the grid is shaded?

☐

Write the decimal number that is equivalent to this fraction.

☐

2 marks

6 1,080 ÷ 9 =

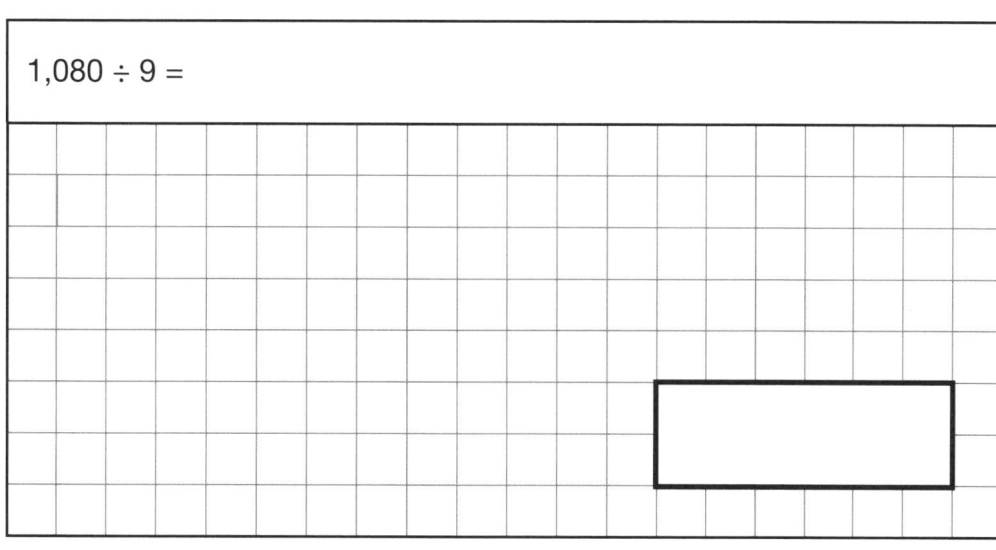

1 mark

[END OF TEST]

Set A Test 11

1 Draw the reflection of the shaded shape using the *x*-axis as the mirror line.

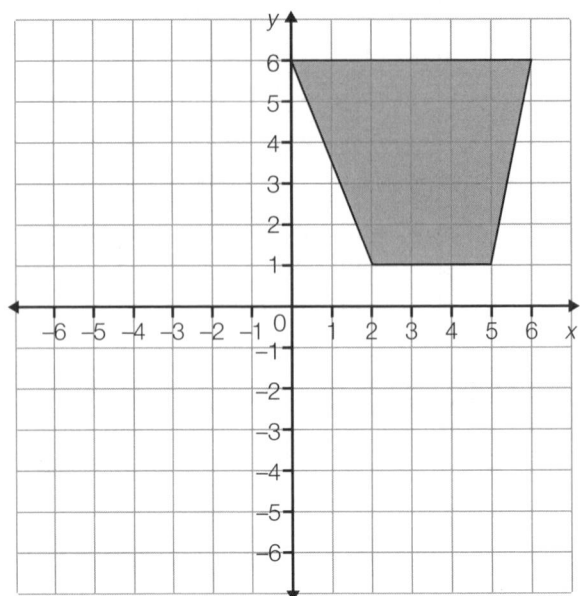

1 mark

2 214.63 − 83.25 =

1 mark

3 Complete the table.

Shape	Number of...		
	Faces	Edges	Vertices
cube	6		
sphere		0	
cylinder			0
triangular prism	5		

2 marks

4 426 × 2 =

1 mark

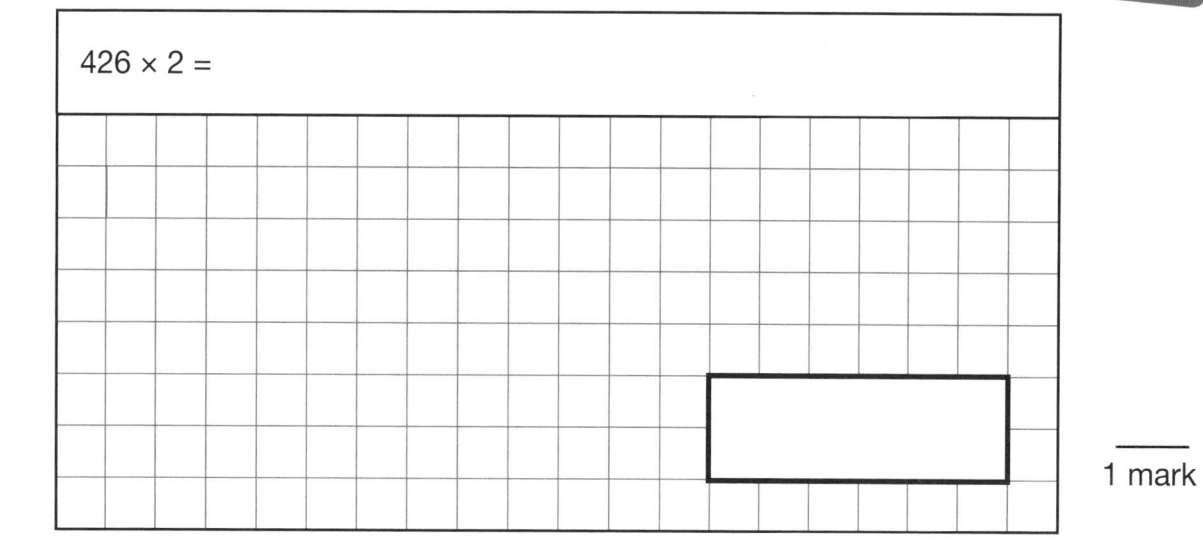

5 Here is an algebraic expression with two variables.

$$2x + y = 8$$

List **all** the possible pairs of positive whole-number values for *x* and *y* in the table.

x			
y			

1 mark

6 $\frac{5}{10} - \frac{2}{5} =$

1 mark

7 Sarah writes a number sequence starting at 270
She subtracts 130 each time.

Write the next two numbers in Sarah's sequence.

| 270 | 140 | 10 | | |

1 mark

Sarah draws a number line.

Write the missing numbers in the boxes.

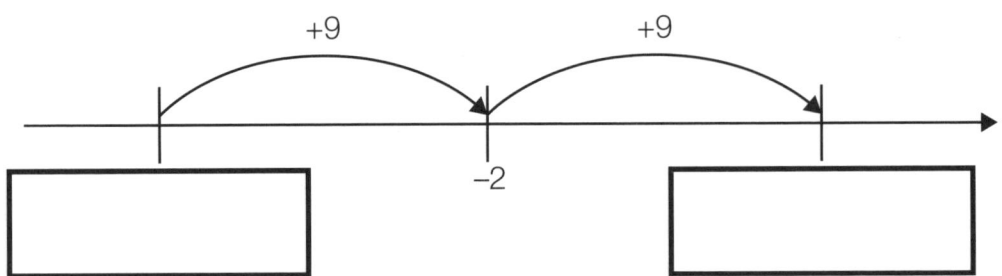

1 mark

8 Write these numbers in order, starting with the **smallest**.

0.3 $\frac{4}{5}$ $\frac{2}{10}$ 0.75

| | | | |

smallest

1 mark

[END OF TEST]

Scoresheet

When you finish the tests in Set A, write your marks in the boxes.

Test 1	/10
Test 2	/10
Test 3	/10
Test 4	/10
Test 5	/10
Test 6	/10
Test 7	/10
Test 8	/10
Test 9	/10
Test 10	/10
Test 11	/10
Total:	/110

How did you do?

0–59

Good start! Practise the topics you found difficult and try to answer the questions in Set A again. Then try Set B.

60–84

Well done! You're already doing well, but practise answering the questions you got wrong in Set A. Then try Set B.

85–110

Great work! You're already doing really well. Look back at the questions you found difficult. Then see if you can do even better in Set B.

A note for parents

Set A is designed to be equivalent to a full set of SATs tests. The exact number of marks students need in order to reach the expected standard in the real tests will vary from year to year. Based on previous assessments, we think students who score 60 or more in Set A are working at or above the expected standard.

Set B Test 1

1 $\frac{20 + x}{4} = 16$

Find the value of **x**.

[   ]

1 mark

2 Here are some metric measurements.

Insert <, > or = in the boxes between them to make the statements correct.

880 ml   8.8 litres

0.01 km   [ ]   1,000 cm

0.15 kg   15 g

1 mark

3 Here is a number pyramid. The number in each box is the **product** of the two numbers below it.

Write the missing numbers.

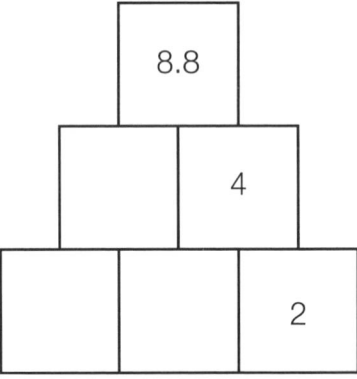

2 marks

4 1,144 ÷ 52 =

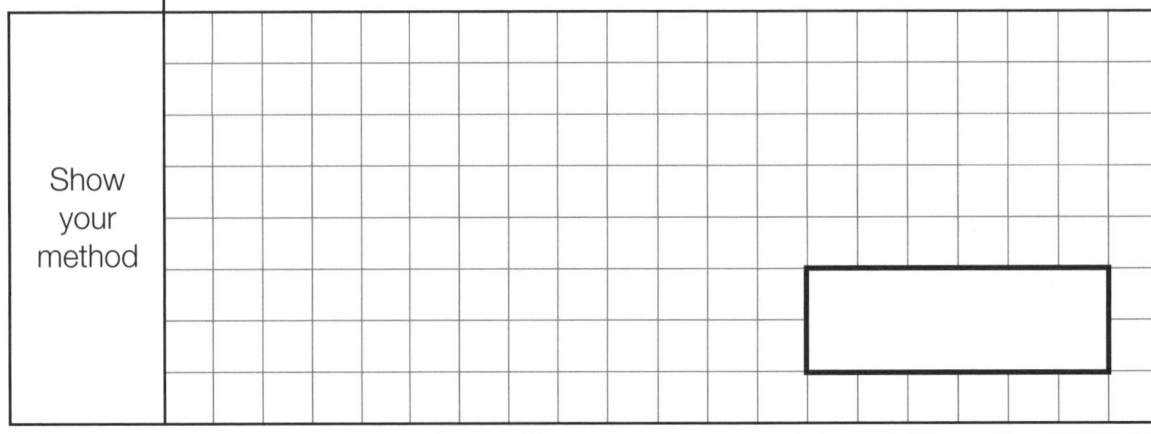

Show your method

2 marks

5 4 × 3 × 9 =

1 mark

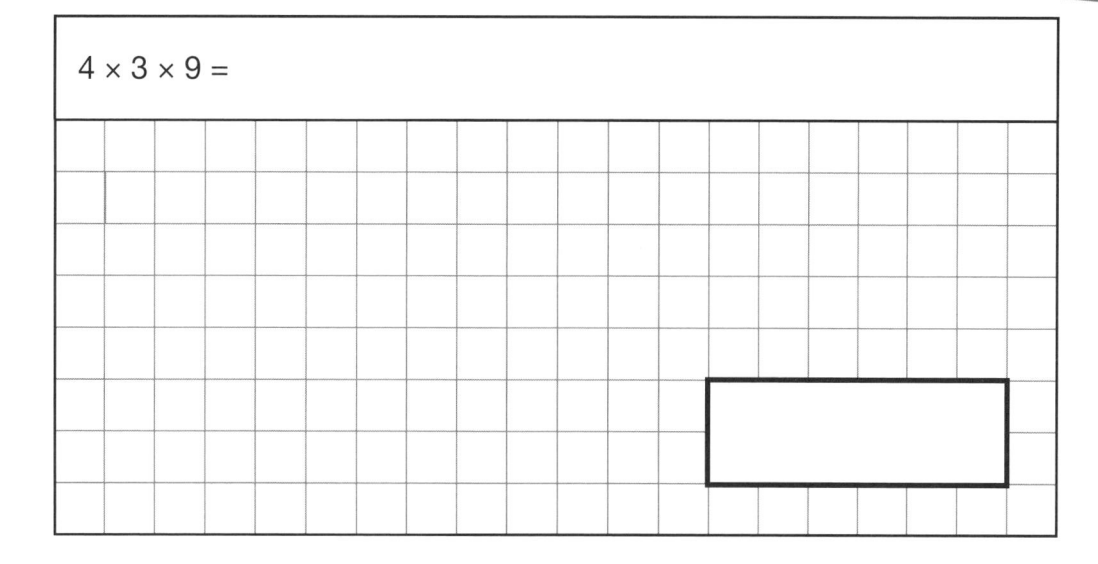

6 180 pupils chose their favourite school meal. 25% chose chicken curry. The remaining children chose fish and chips.

How many more children chose fish and chips than chose chicken curry?

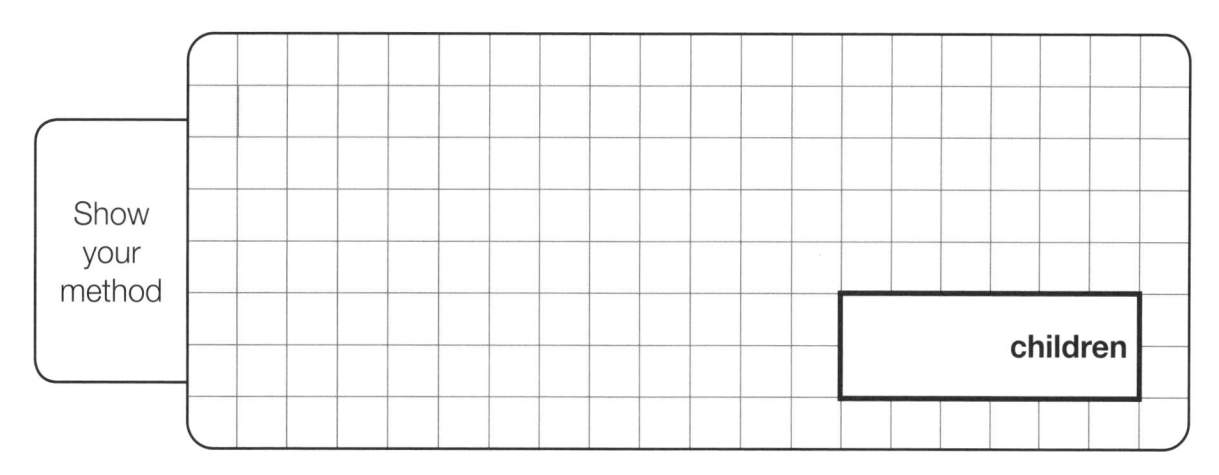

Show your method

children

2 marks

7 1,031 − 9 =

1 mark

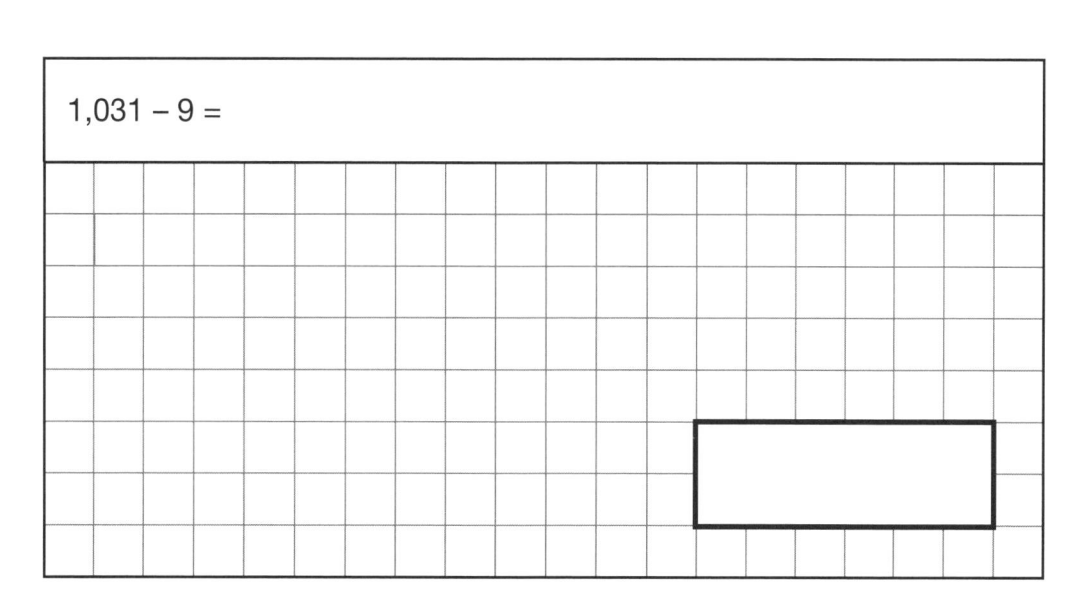

[END OF TEST]

Set B Test 2

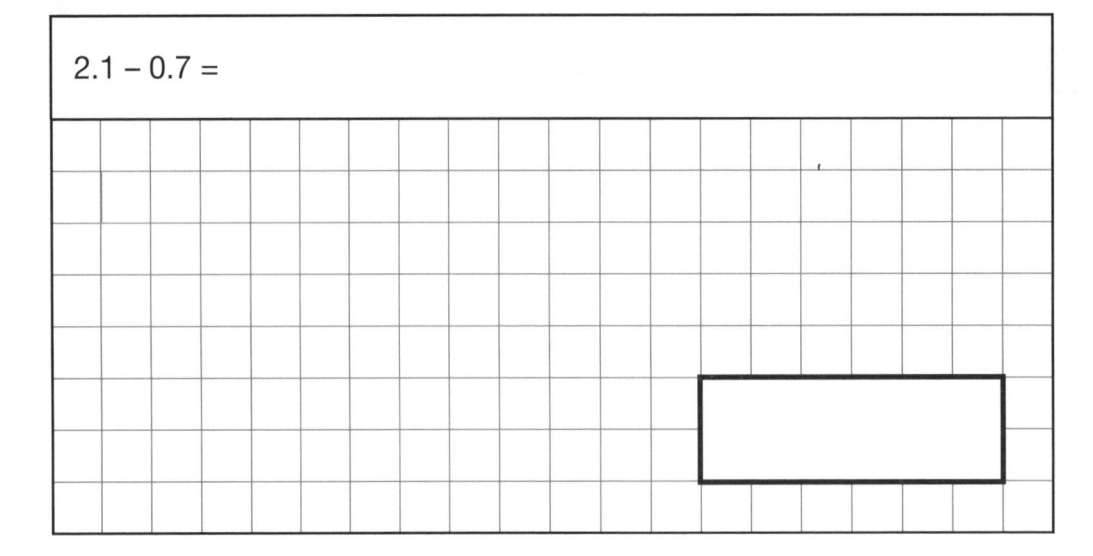

1. 2.1 − 0.7 =

1 mark

2. Sofiyan has four different types of coin represented by the four different shapes below. He adds pairs together. The totals are shown in pence.

Find the value of each coin.

○	+	▭	=	7p
△	÷	○	=	10p
▭	+	▭	=	10p
◇	−	△	=	30p

○ = ____ p   △ = ____ p

▭ = ____ p   ◇ = ____ p

2 marks

3 Write the four missing digits to make this **subtraction** correct.

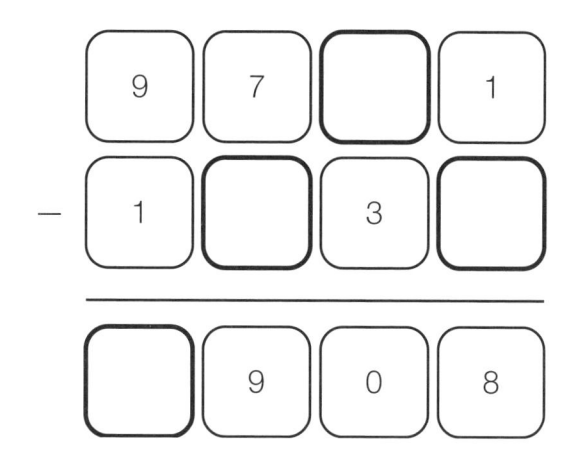

$$\begin{array}{r} 9\;7\;\square\;1 \\ -\;\;1\;\square\;3\;\square \\ \hline \square\;9\;0\;8 \end{array}$$

2 marks

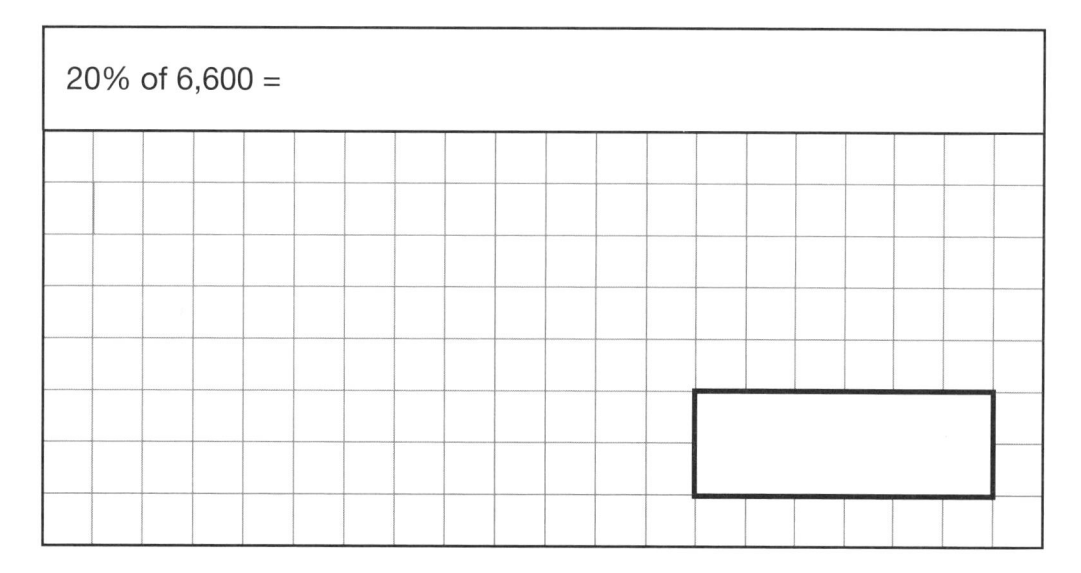

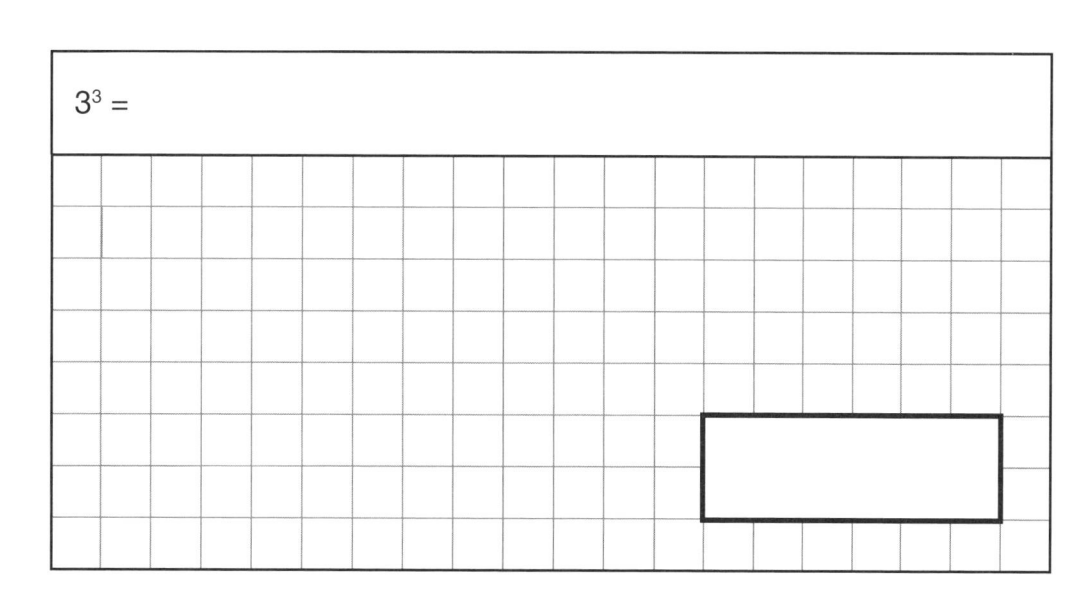

4 20% of 6,600 =

1 mark

5 $3^3 =$

1 mark

Set B Test 2

6 Here is a parallelogram.

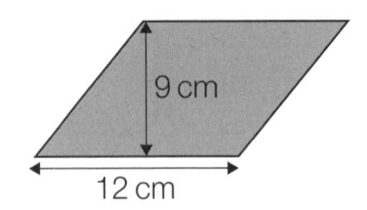

9 cm

12 cm

Calculate the area of the parallelogram.

cm²

1 mark

On the grid, draw a parallelogram that has the same area as the shaded triangle.

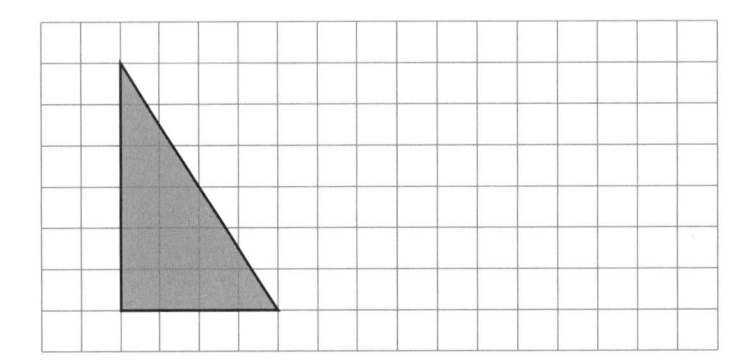

1 mark

7 $1\frac{6}{10} + \frac{4}{20} =$

1 mark

[END OF TEST]

Set B Test 3

1 Green Wood School organises a cake sale. Each cupcake costs £1.25
The children decide to give $\frac{1}{5}$ of the money to charity.

If the school sells 100 cupcakes, how much money would be given to the charity?

£ ☐

1 mark

If the charity receives £10, how many cupcakes were sold?

☐

1 mark

2 Guy measures a paper clip against a ruler.

How long is the paper clip in millimetres?

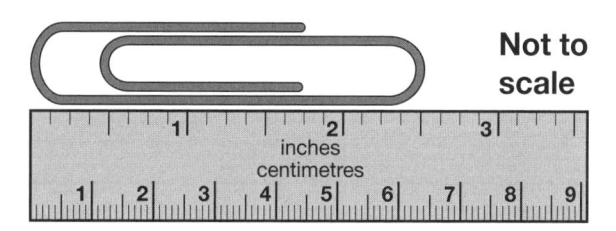

Not to scale

☐ mm

1 mark

Guy puts five paper clips horizontally end to end.

How long is the line of paper clips in inches?

☐ inches

1 mark

3 $\frac{5}{12} + \frac{1}{6} =$

☐

1 mark

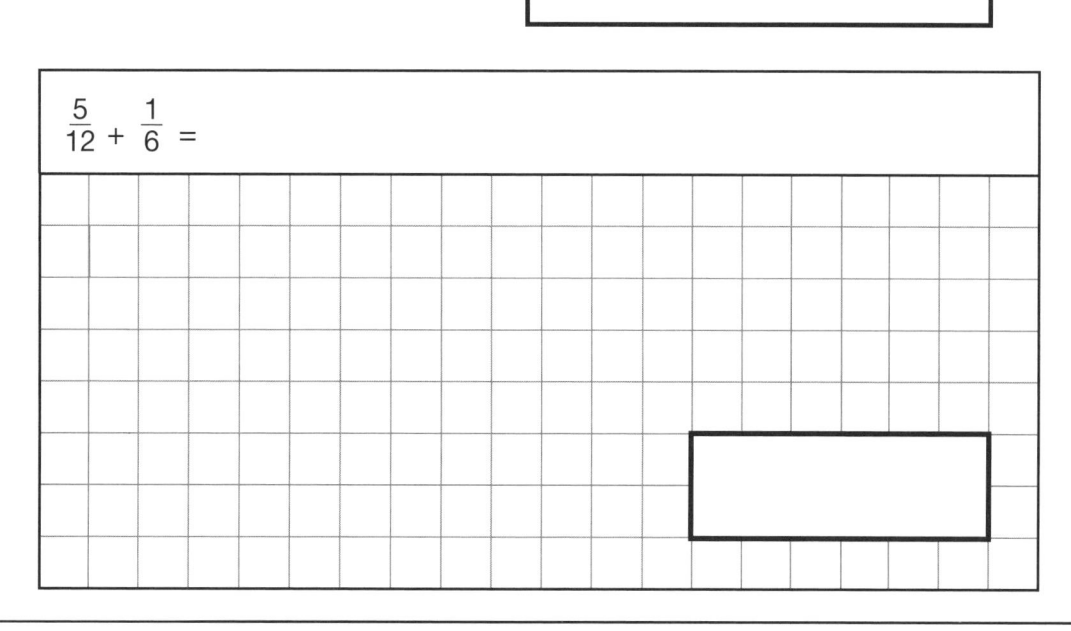

Set B Test 3

4 Thames Class play Avon Class in the house football tournament.
The final score is 2–1

What were **all** the possible scores at half-time?

Thames Class	Avon Class

2 marks

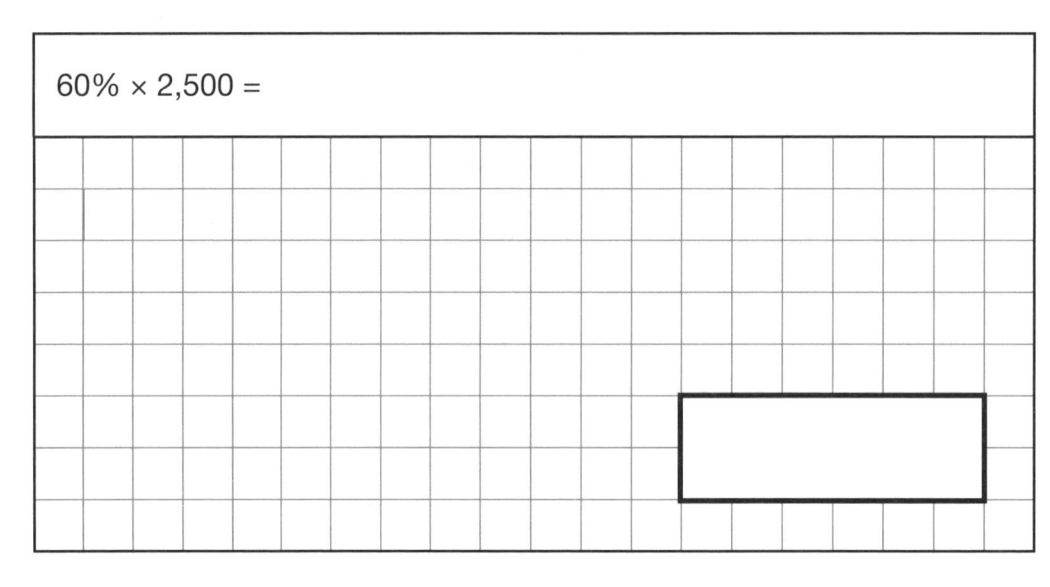

5 60% × 2,500 =

1 mark

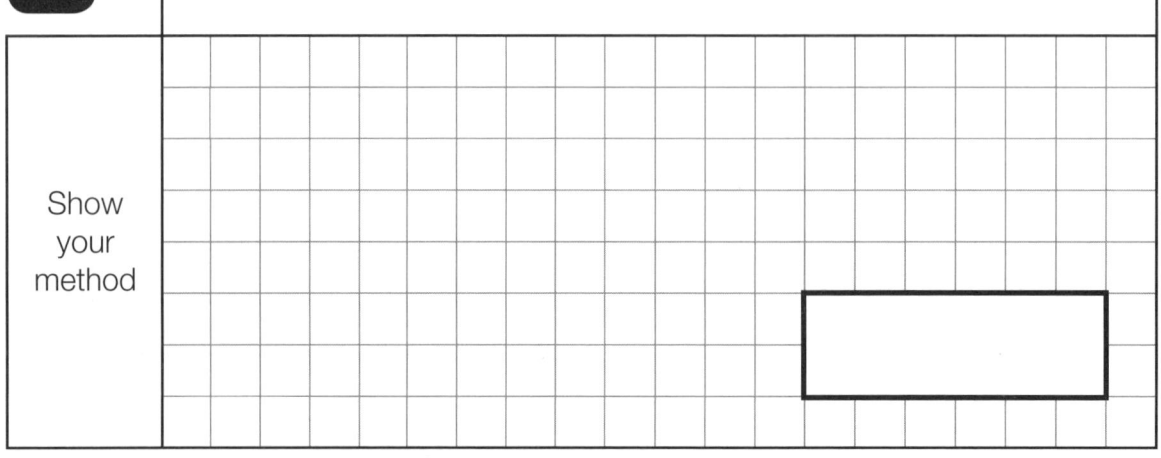

6 432 × 33 =

Show your method

2 marks

[END OF TEST]

Set B Test 4

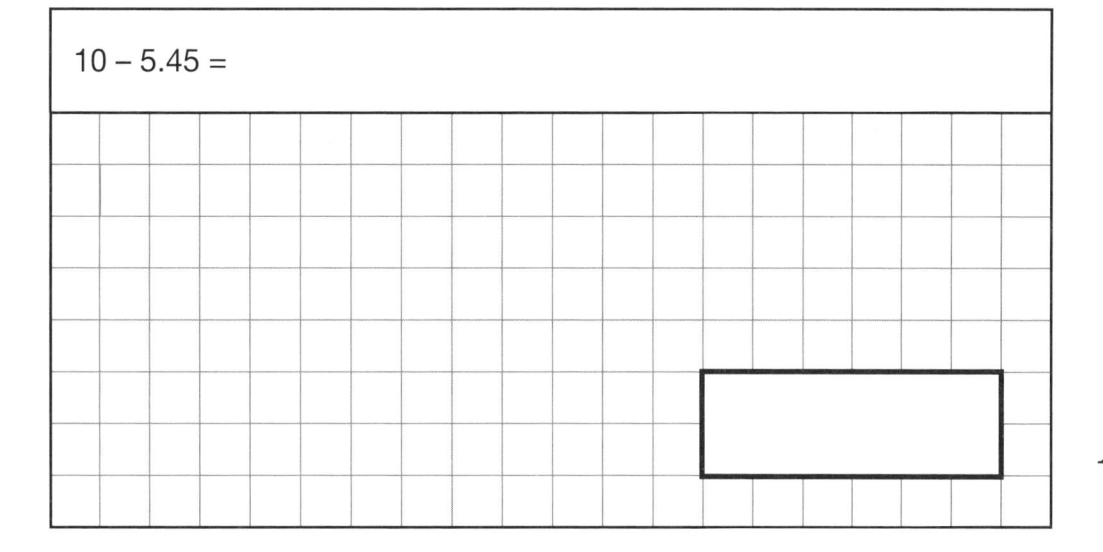

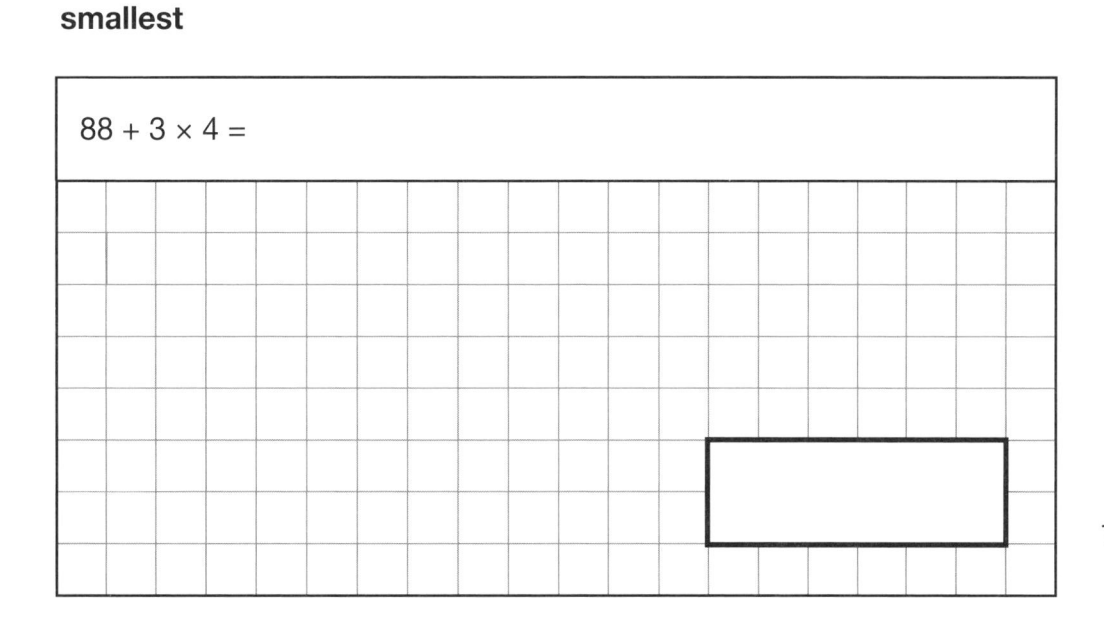

1 10 − 5.45 =

_____
1 mark

2 Write these measurements in order, starting with the **smallest**.

10.01 cm   110 mm   0.01 m   1.01 m   10 cm

smallest

_____
1 mark

3 88 + 3 × 4 =

_____
1 mark

4 In a test, Mo got 40% correct and Jasmine got 75%. The test was out of 60 marks.

What was Mo's score out of 60?

_____
1 mark

How many more marks did Jasmine get than Mo?

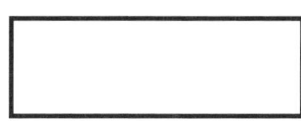

_____
1 mark

Set B Test 4

4 Colour in four more hexagons on this grid so that the grey pattern is reflected in the mirror line.

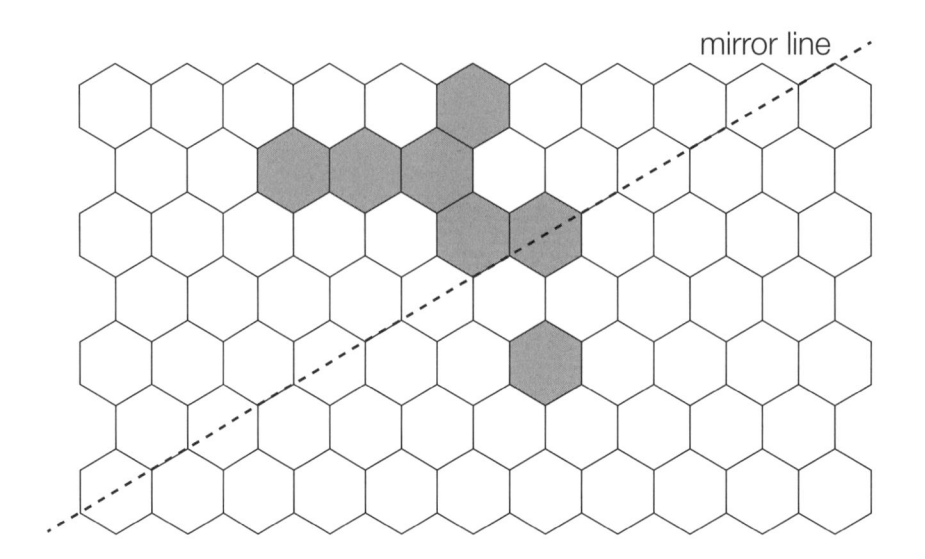

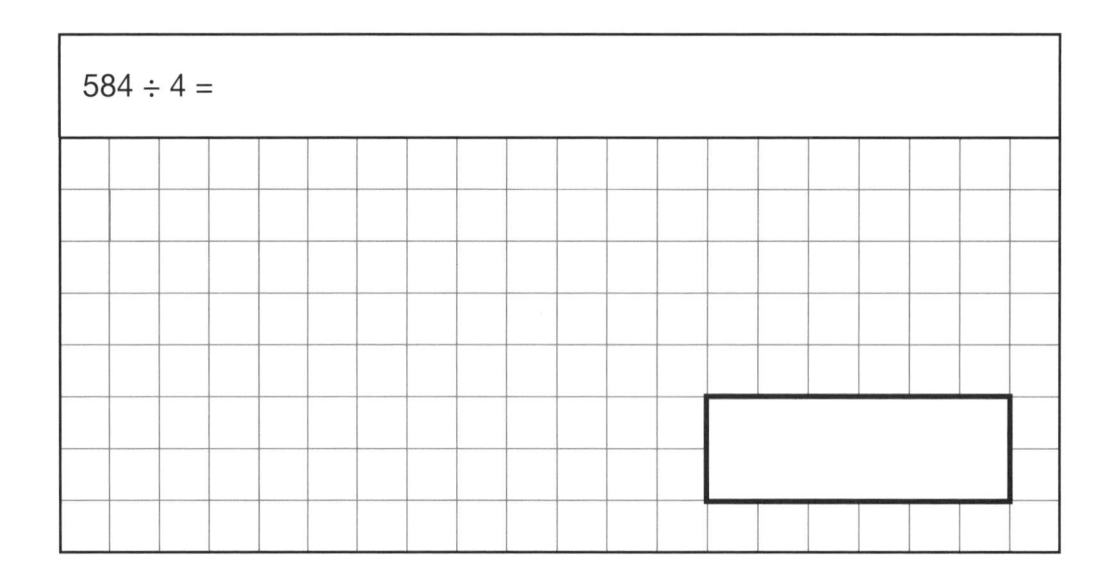

mirror line

2 marks

5 Circle **all** the numbers that make 50 when rounded to the nearest 10.

41.22   53.99   49.15   55.50   45.01

1 mark

6 584 ÷ 4 =

1 mark

7 Here are four fraction cards.

$\frac{2}{5}$ $\frac{9}{15}$ $\frac{2}{10}$ $\frac{16}{20}$

Write one fraction in each box to make the statement correct.

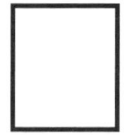

☐ > ☐ > ☐ > ☐

1 mark

[END OF TEST]

Set B Test 5

1 Waseem makes a model using red and green bricks. He uses 5 red bricks for every 3 green bricks he uses. He uses 120 bricks altogether.

How many green bricks does he use?

☐ bricks

1 mark

2 483,927 − 56,884 =

☐

1 mark

3 Maisie goes swimming regularly and records her workouts.

Number of lengths in session	Average time per length (seconds)
7	21.5
9	17.5
10	20.5
9	21.0
11	17.5
8	16.5

What is the **mean** number of lengths Maisie swims?

☐

1 mark

What is her **mean** time per length when she swims more than nine lengths?

☐

1 mark

Set B Test 5

4 1,009 − 100 =

1 mark

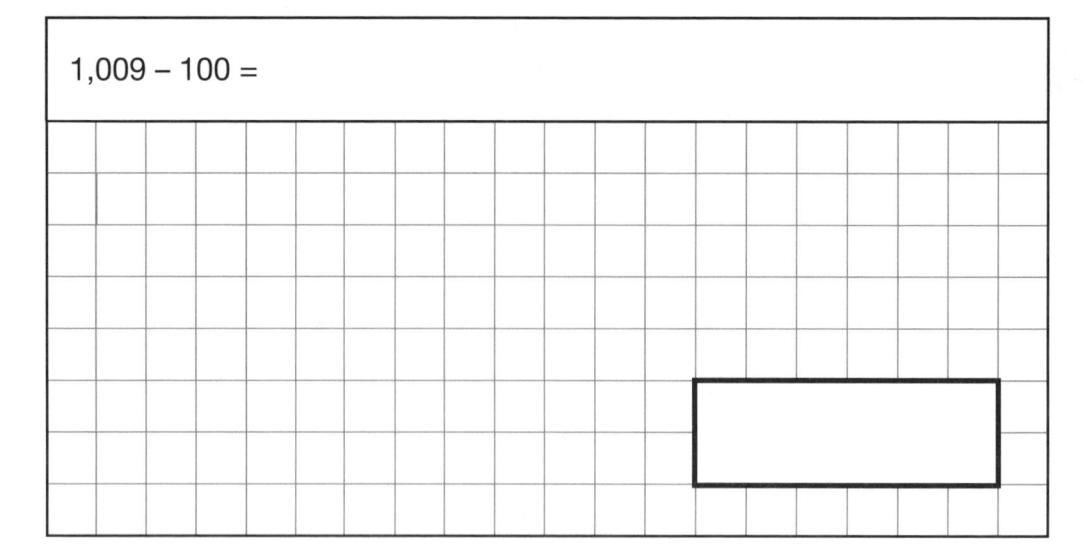

5 Circle **all** the numbers that are equivalent to each other.

$\frac{3}{5}$ 0.6 $\frac{12}{20}$ $\frac{6}{8}$ $\frac{8}{16}$ 0.8

1 mark

6 127 × 82 =

Show your method

2 marks

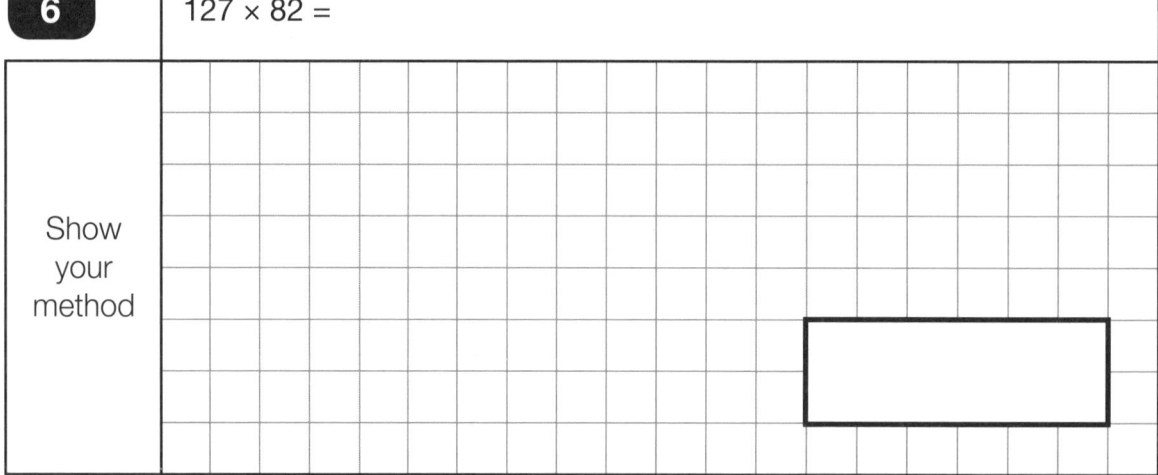

7 9 and 16 are both square numbers.

They have a sum of 25

Find two square numbers that have a sum that is four times larger.

2 marks

[END OF TEST]

Set B Test 6

1 983 + 100 =

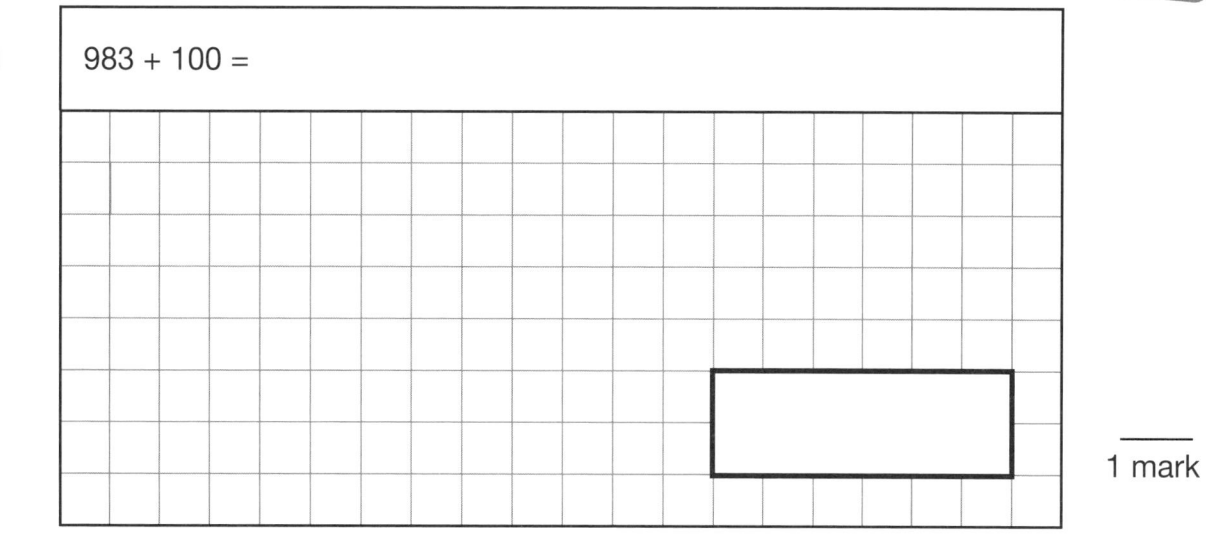

1 mark

2 Annie draws the nets for two cuboids, A and B, on centimetre-squared paper.

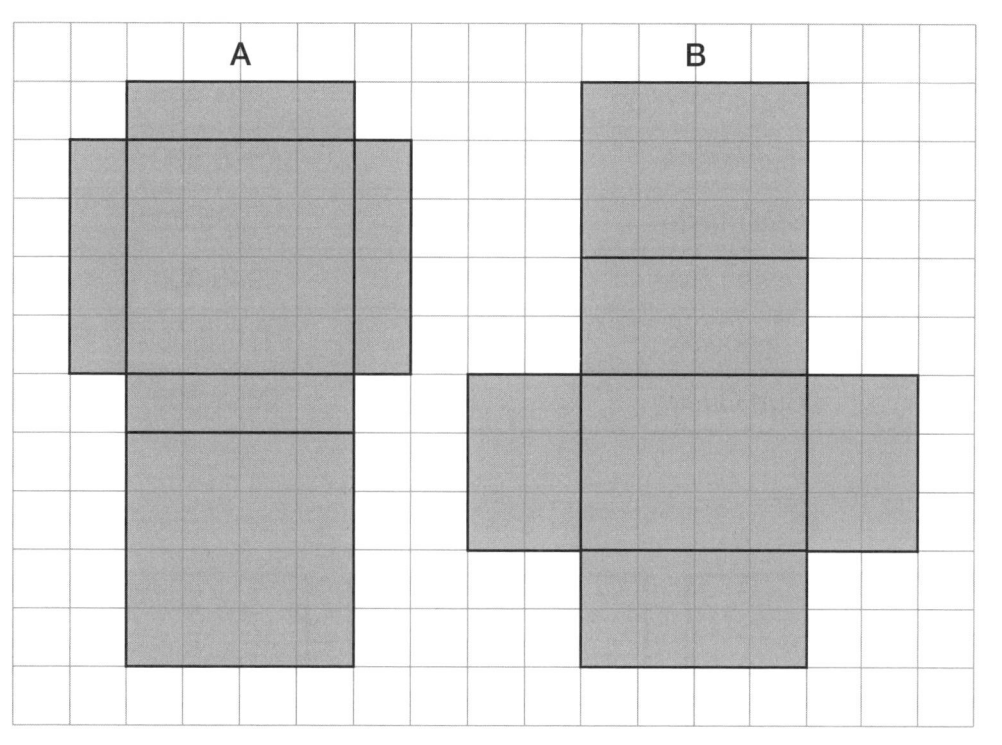

Not to scale

Which cuboid has the larger **volume**?

1 mark

What is the difference in **volume** between the two cuboids?

cm³

1 mark

Set B Test 6

3 $\frac{7}{10} \div 10 =$

1 mark

4 Cameron's dad is buying a new boat. He is looking at yachts that cost between £950,000 and £1,050,000. Here are his choices.

Yacht	Price
Spirit of the Wind	£905,999
Explorer II	£990,500
Sea Master	£1,005,000
Ocean Bliss	£945,500
Velocité	£1,115,000
Sun Queen	£951,000

Name the three yachts he looks at.

1 mark

5 91 × 7 =

1 mark

6 $P = S - (C + T)$ (where P = profit, S = total sales, C = costs and T = taxes)

Write out the meaning of this formula in words.

_____

_____

1 mark

7 Whiteboard pens are sold in packs of 12
The head teacher needs to order a pen for every child in her school of 250 children.

How many packs must she buy?

[ ] packs

1 mark

How many spare pens are left over after she has given a pen to each child?

[ ] pens

1 mark

8 $5^2 =$

1 mark

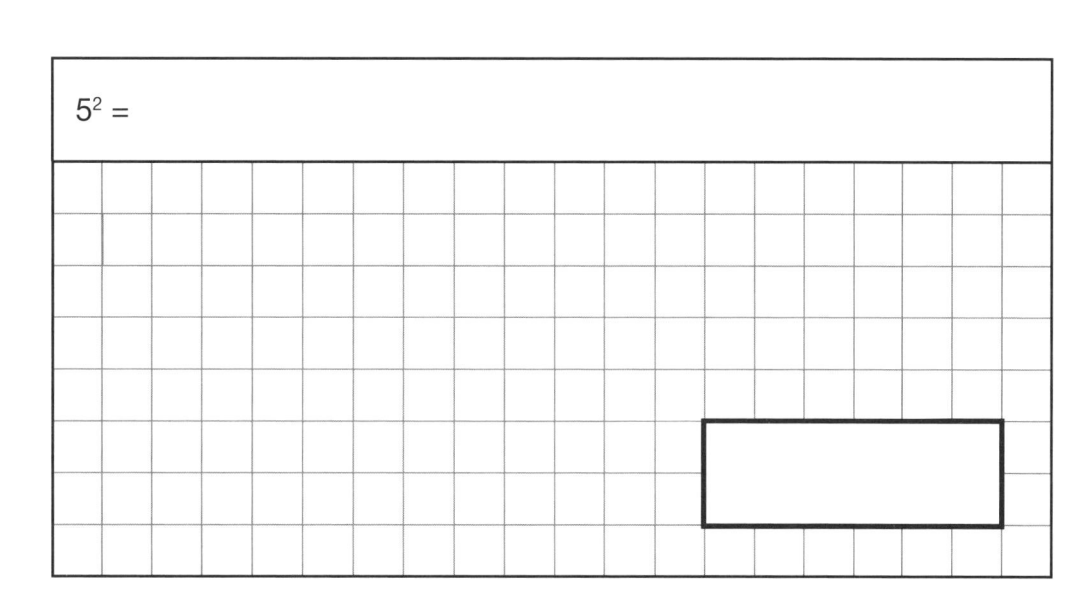

[END OF TEST]

Set B Test 7

1 999 + 11 =

1 mark

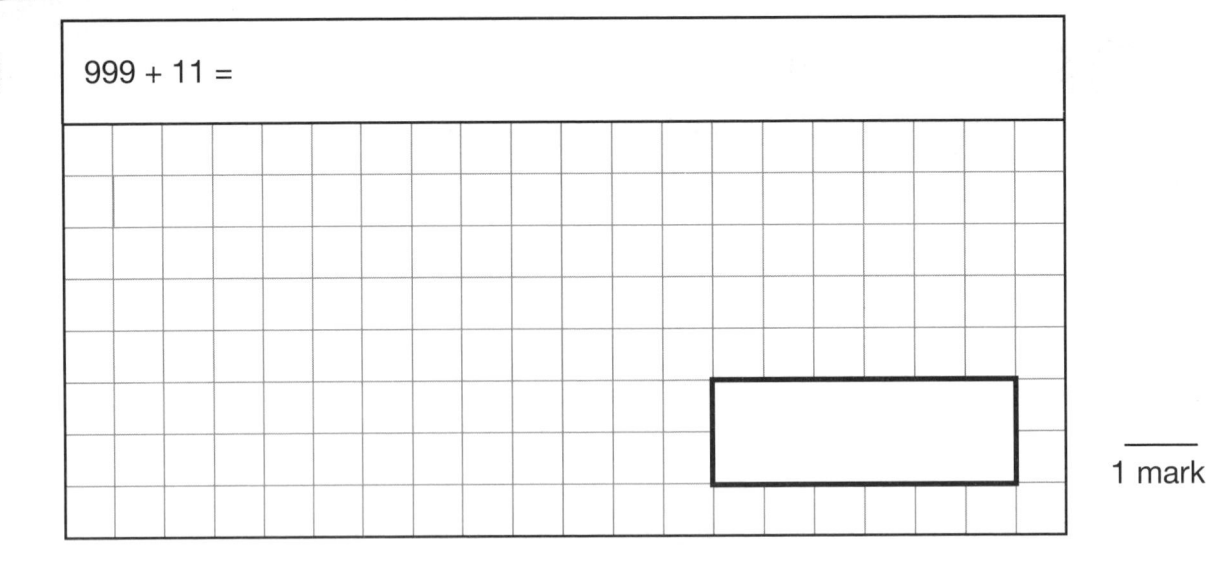

2 Here is a chart of the rate of rainfall and the temperature in Tropical City over 24 hours.

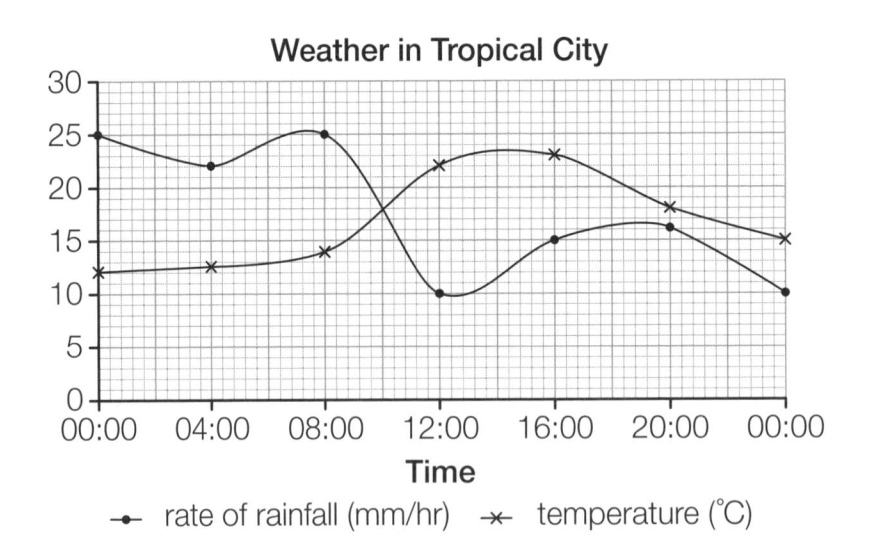

Weather in Tropical City

— rate of rainfall (mm/hr)   ✳ temperature (°C)

Between which hours did the rate of rainfall decrease the fastest?

[ ] and [ ]

1 mark

For how many hours was the temperature 18 °C or above?

[ ] hours

1 mark

3 720 ÷ 8 =

1 mark

4 Here are three number cards.

3　6　1

Choose two cards each time to make the following two-digit numbers.

the square of 4		
a common multiple of 3 and 12		
a common factor of 26 and 130		
a prime number greater than 20		

2 marks

5 90% of 360 =

1 mark

Set B Test 7

6 Three decimal numbers add together to equal 1
The first number is 0.09
The second number is 0.4

What is the third number?

1 mark

Three fractions add together to equal 1
The first fraction is $\frac{15}{30}$ and the second fraction is $\frac{2}{8}$

What is the third fraction in its simplest form?

1 mark

7 This scale shows how much Tamir weighs.

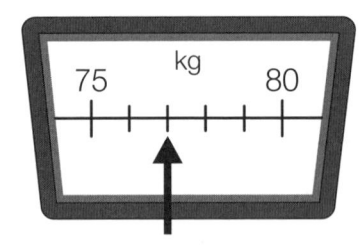

Here is a new scale.

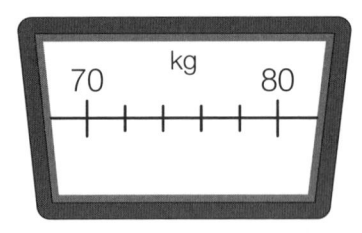

Mark Tamir's weight on the new scale with an arrow.

1 mark

[END OF TEST]

Set B Test 8

1 Aliysha says,

"When you divide a whole number by another whole number, the answer will always be smaller than either of the two numbers you started with."

Aliysha is wrong.

Explain how you know.

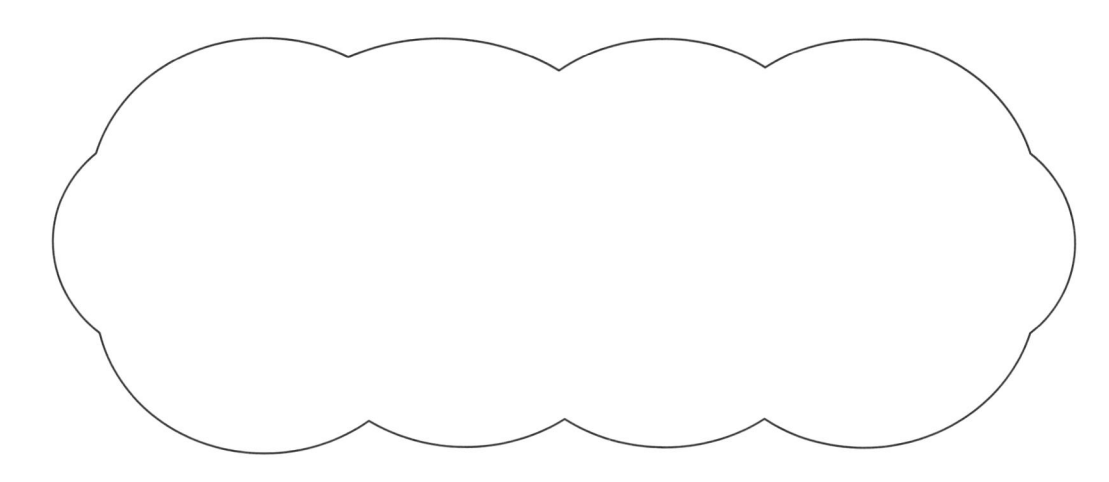

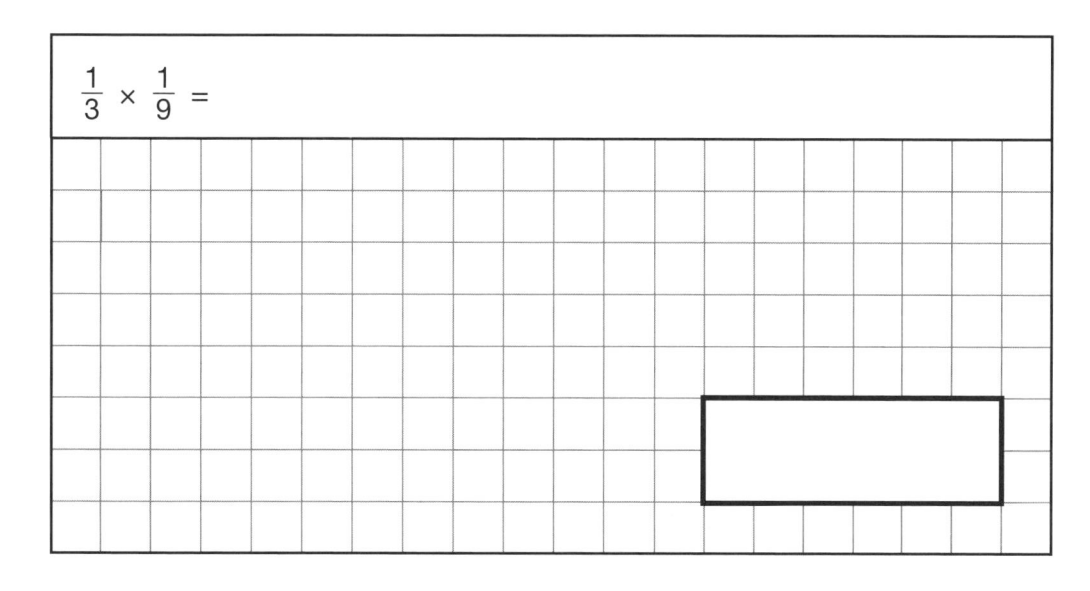

_____
1 mark

2 $\frac{1}{3} \times \frac{1}{9} =$

_____
1 mark

3 Complete this number sequence.

60   50   41   _____   26   _____   15

_____
1 mark

4 Here is a scalene triangle.

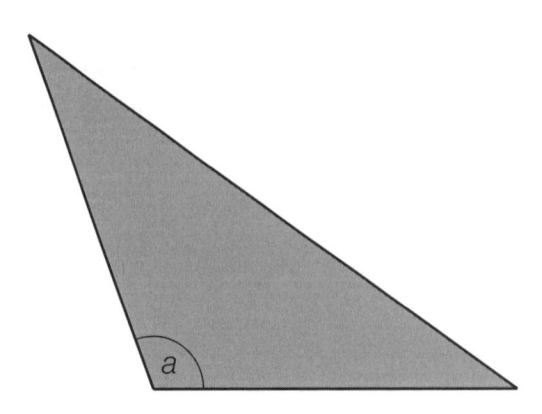

a

What type of angle is angle *a*? Circle the correct answer.

reflex   obtuse   acute   right-angle

1 mark

Measure angle *a* accurately. Use a protractor.

☐ °

1 mark

5 744 ÷ 24 =

Show your method

2 marks

6 27,415 + 4,725 =

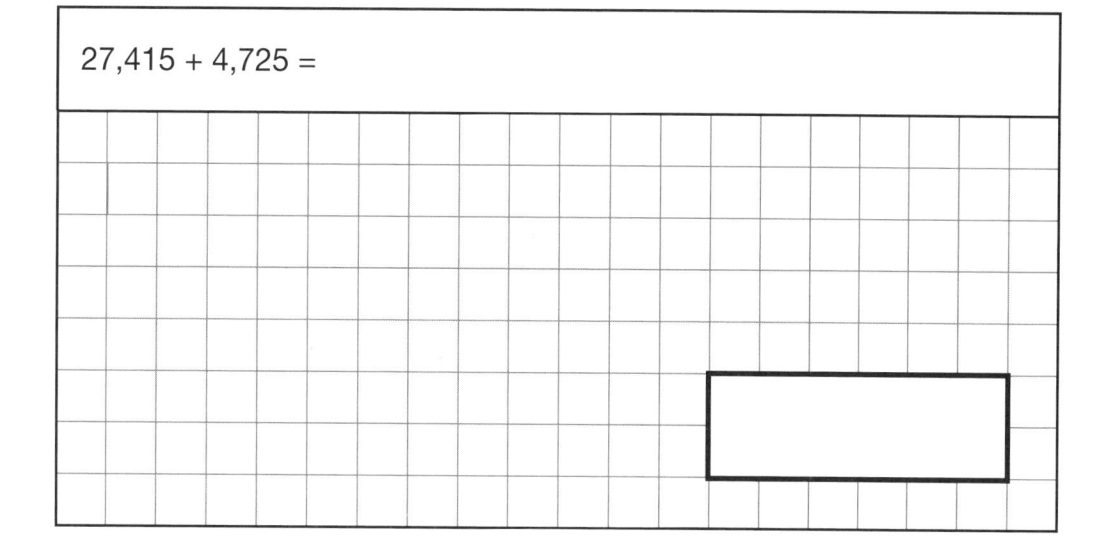

1 mark

7 This quadrilateral has sides of length:

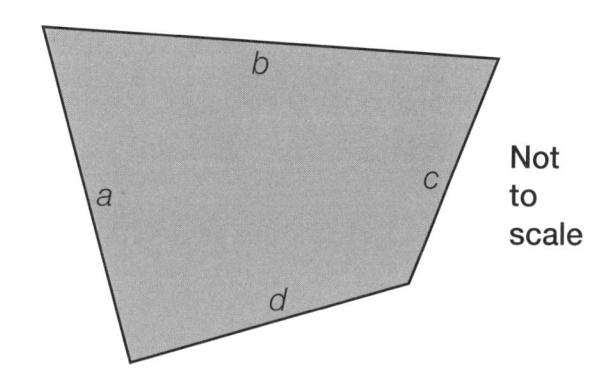

a = 5 cm   b = 7 cm   c = 3 cm   d = 4 cm

Not to scale

Complete the table to show the lengths of the sides after the shape has been enlarged by different scale factors.

Scale factor	a	b	c	d
3	15 cm			
$\frac{1}{2}$				2 cm

2 marks

[END OF TEST]

Set B Test 9

1 7.9 + 0.6 =

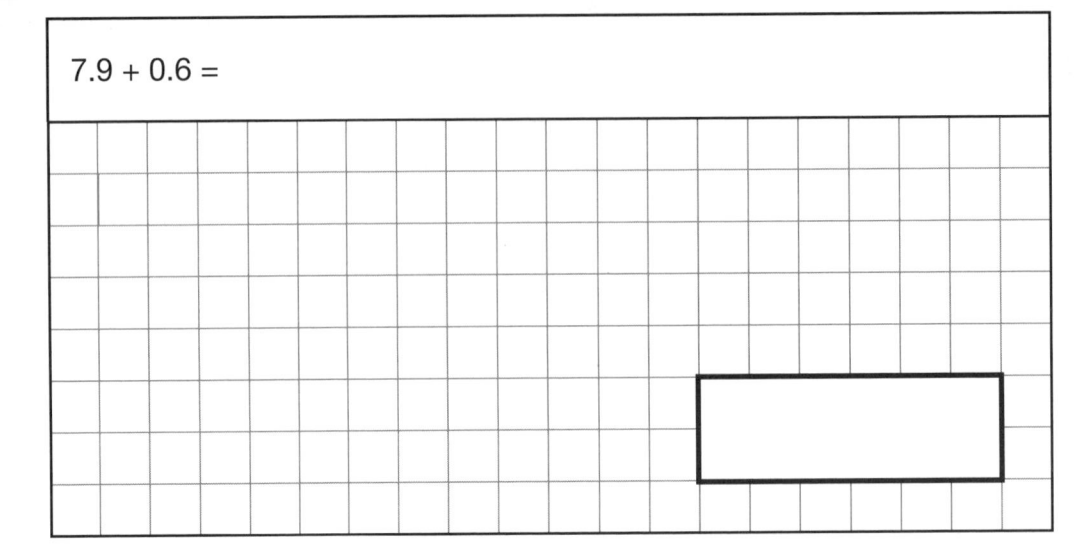

1 mark

2 Some of this grid is shaded.

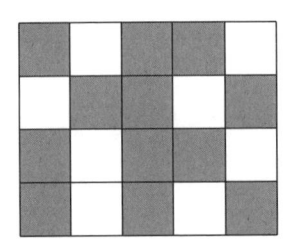

What is the equivalent shaded amount as a percentage?

___ %

1 mark

3 Complete this drawing of a 3D cube by drawing four more lines on the grid.

Use a ruler.

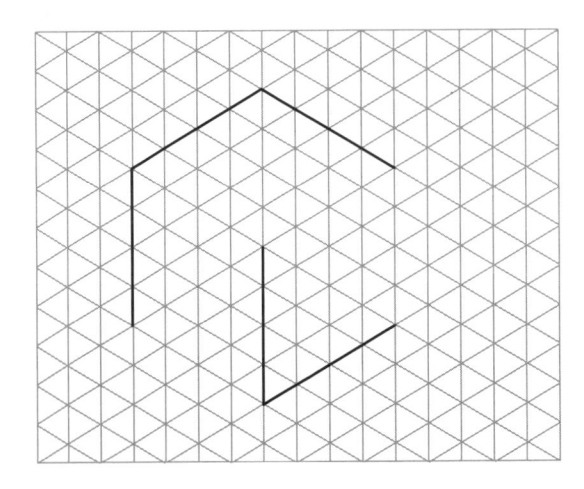

1 mark

4 62 × 24 =

Show your method

2 marks

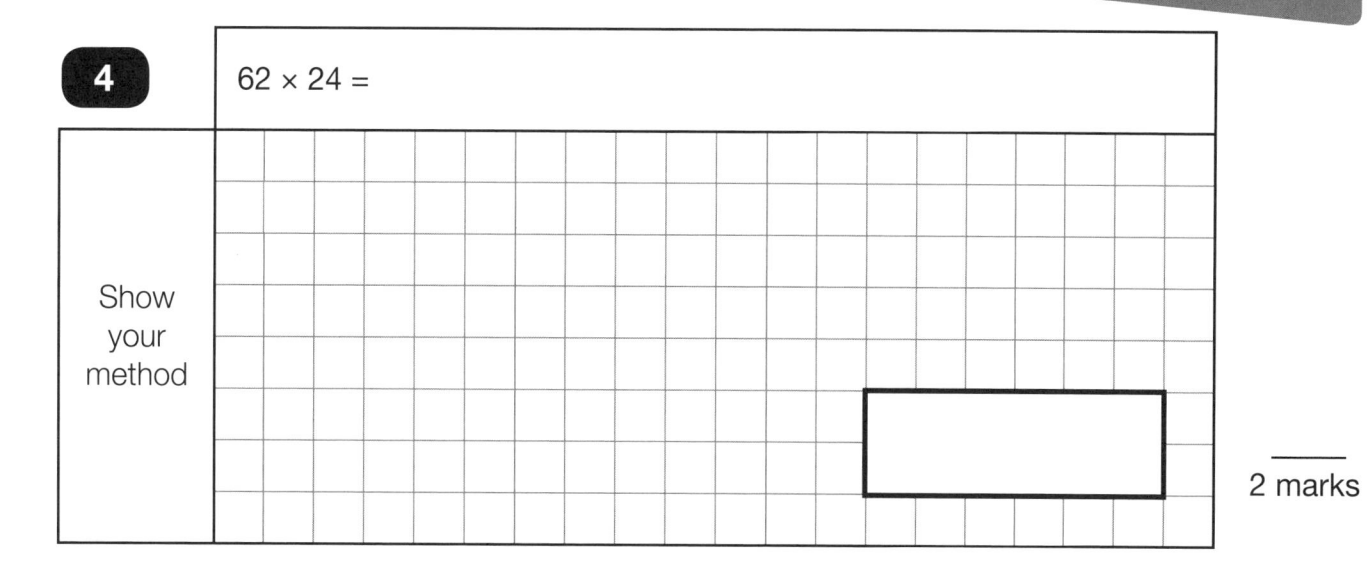

5 Match the times to the equivalent 24-hour clock times.

One has been done for you.

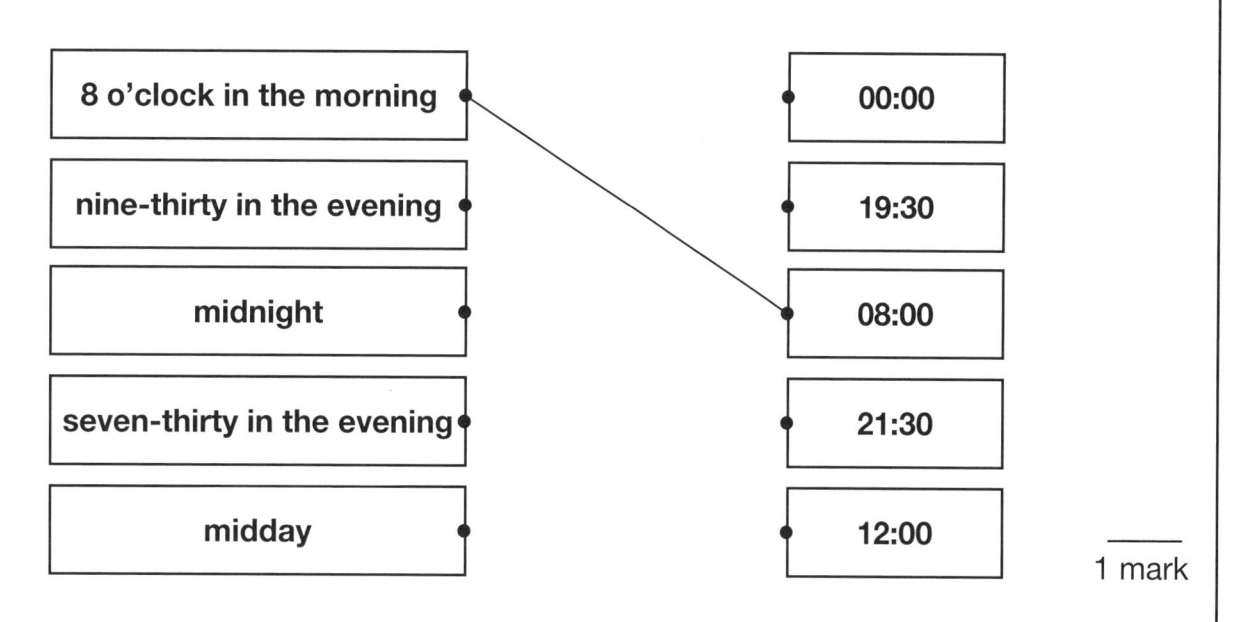

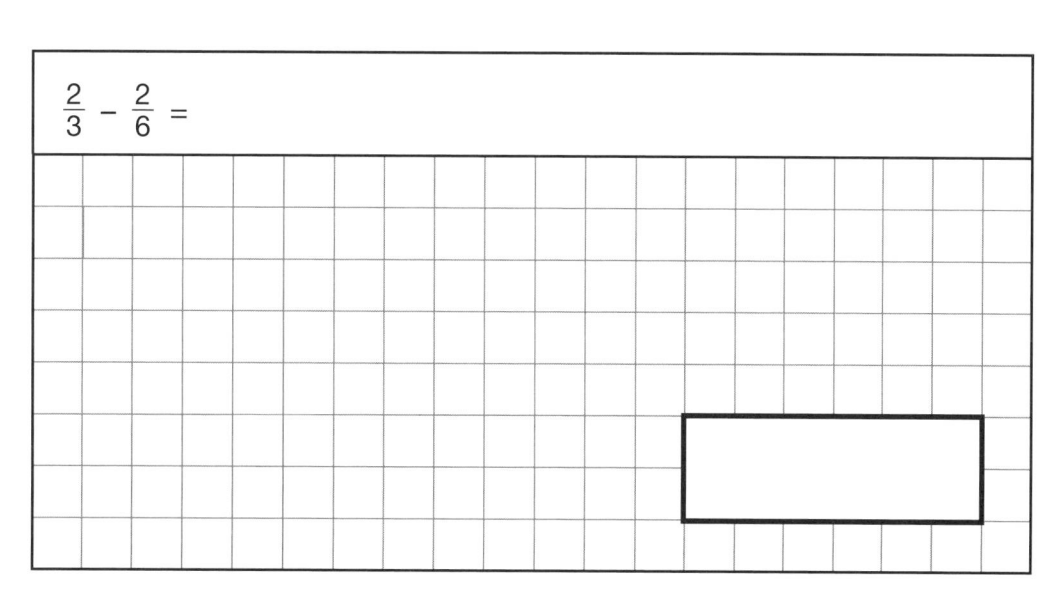

8 o'clock in the morning	—	00:00
nine-thirty in the evening		19:30
midnight		08:00
seven-thirty in the evening		21:30
midday		12:00

1 mark

6 $\frac{2}{3} - \frac{2}{6} =$

1 mark

Set B Test 9

7 Emily and Joe each buy a fruit smoothie.
Joe receives 15p change from £3
Emily receives £1.05 change from £5

How much less does Joe pay than Emily?

Show your method

£ ⬜

2 marks

8 Here are four number cards.

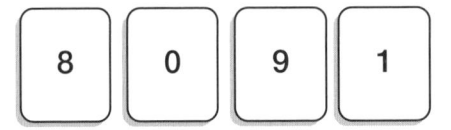

| 8 | 0 | 9 | 1 |

Use each card once only to make the number nearest to 90

⬜ ⬜ . ⬜ ⬜

1 mark

[END OF TEST]

1 This bar chart shows how much money some people have in their bank accounts. This is called their bank balance.
Some of the people have some money. Their balances are positive.
Other people owe some money. Their balances are negative.

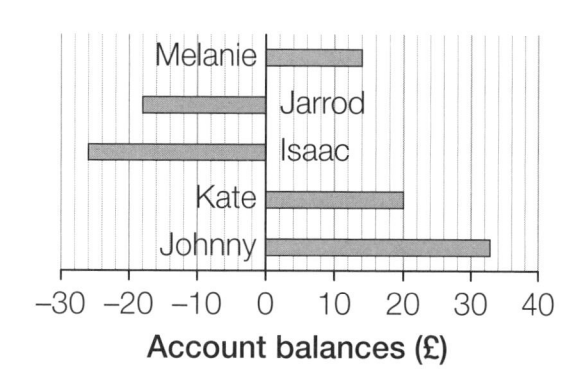

How much more money does Kate have than Jarrod?

£ ☐

1 mark

Which person has 40 fewer pounds than Melanie?

☐

1 mark

2 0.981 × 100 =

1 mark

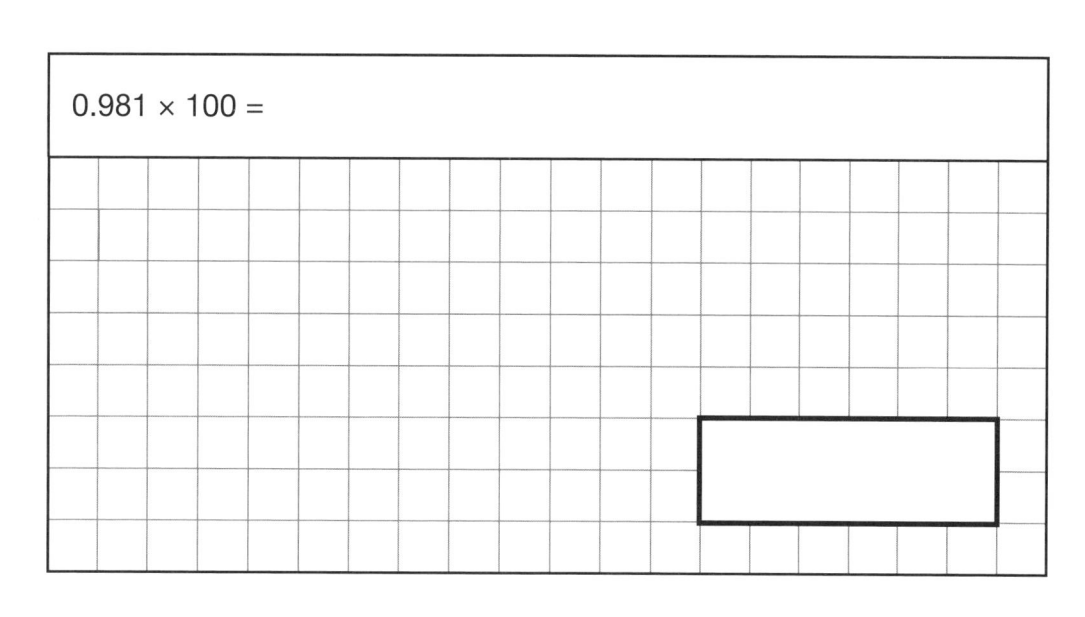

Set B Test 10

3 120 people were asked where they went on holiday.

United Kingdom	Italy	Spain	Greece	France
50	5	30	10	25

Complete the pie chart below to show this data in full. Draw lines and write labels.

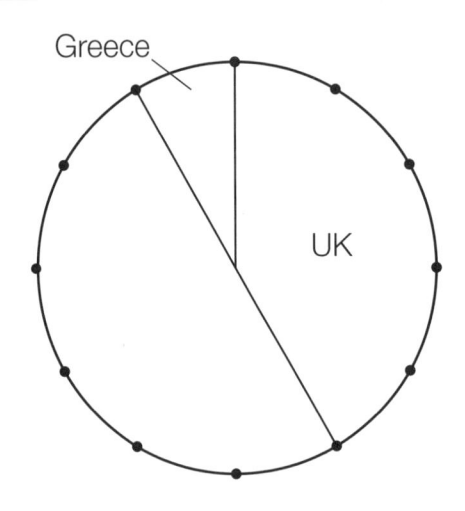

2 marks

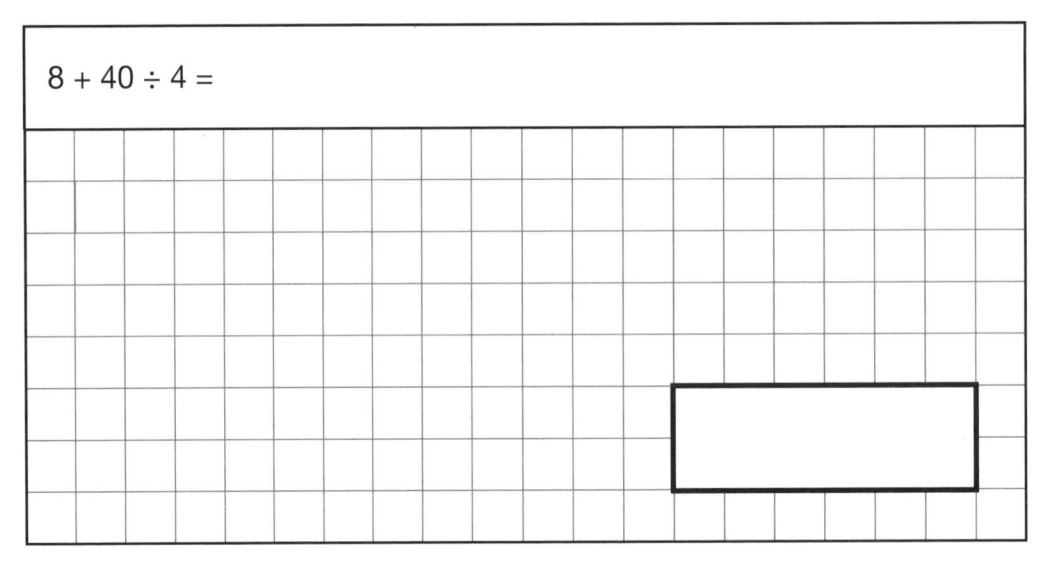

4 8 + 40 ÷ 4 =

1 mark

5 $25 \times 2\frac{1}{2} =$

1 mark

56

6 Here are some 2D shapes.

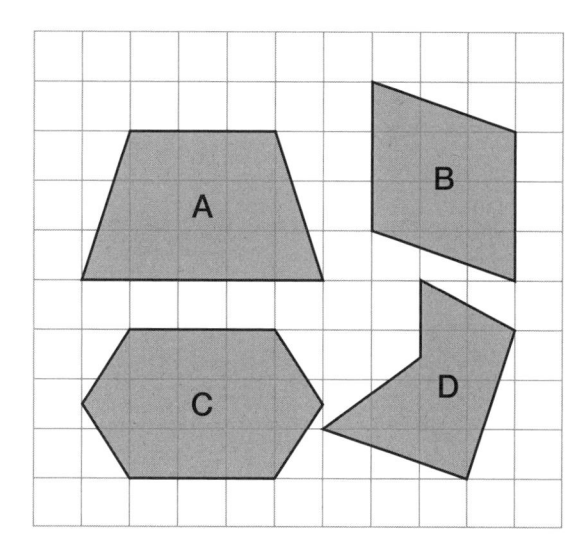

Write the letter of each shape that has more than one pair of parallel sides.

1 mark

7 Stick A and Stick B measure 70 cm when placed end to end. Stick B is four times as long as Stick A.

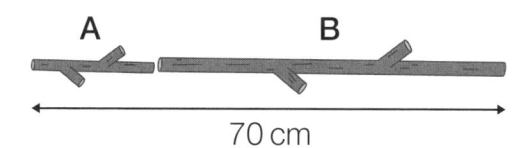

How long is Stick B?

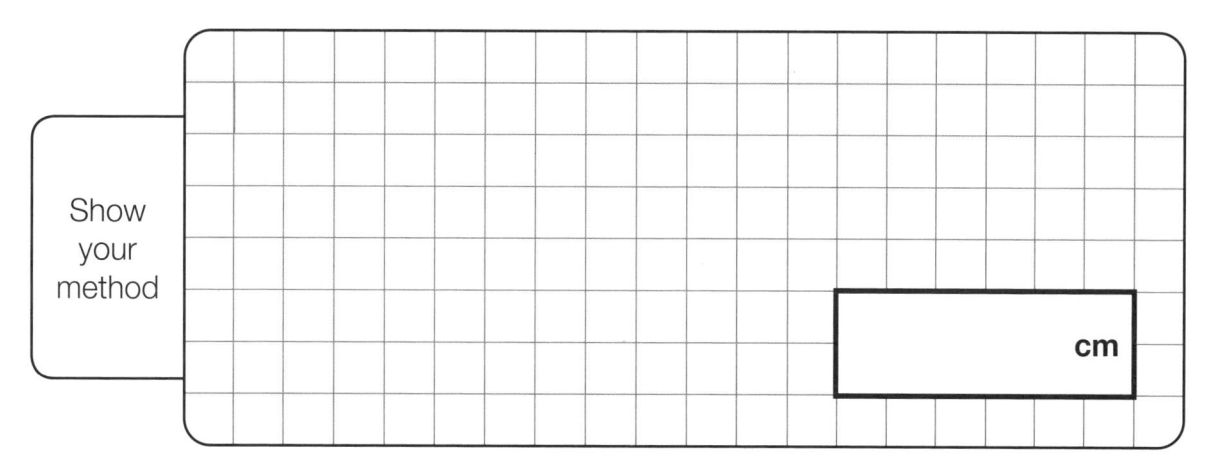

Show your method

cm

2 marks

[END OF TEST]

Set B Test 11

1 2.43 × 7 =

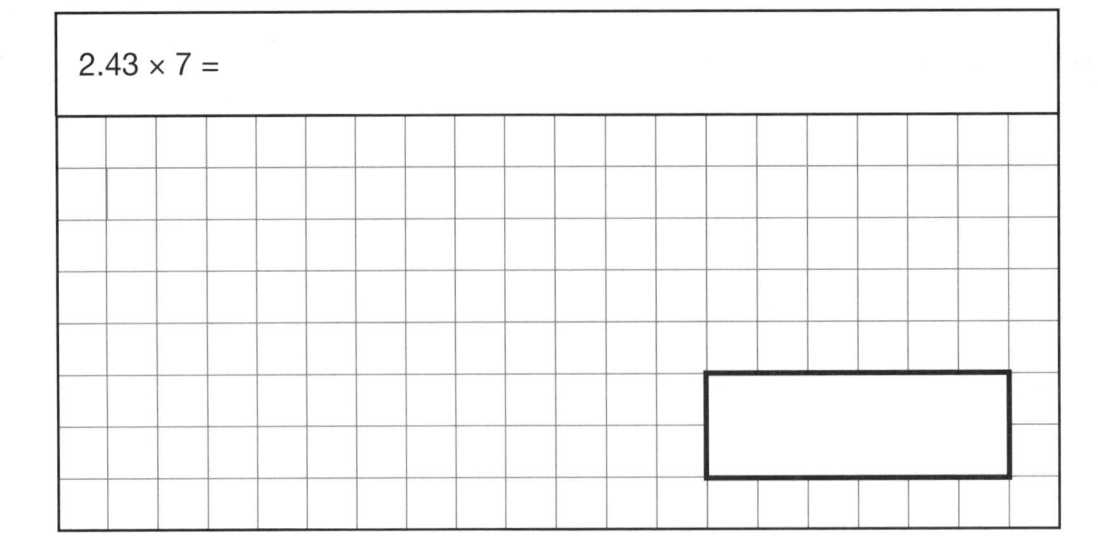

1 mark

2 Monty has the same number of 5p and 20p coins.
He has £3.75 altogether.

How many of each coin does he have?

of each coin

1 mark

3 $\frac{2}{3} \times 4 =$

1 mark

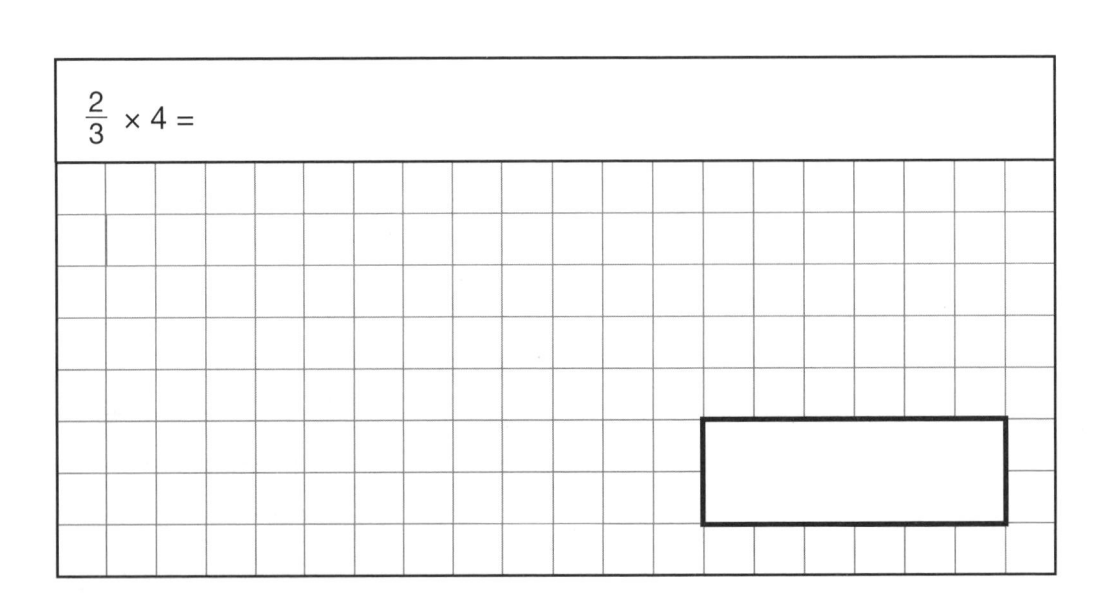

4 Circle the fractions that are equivalent to 0.75

$\frac{3}{4}$ $\frac{8}{12}$ $\frac{1}{75}$ $\frac{75}{100}$ $\frac{33}{44}$

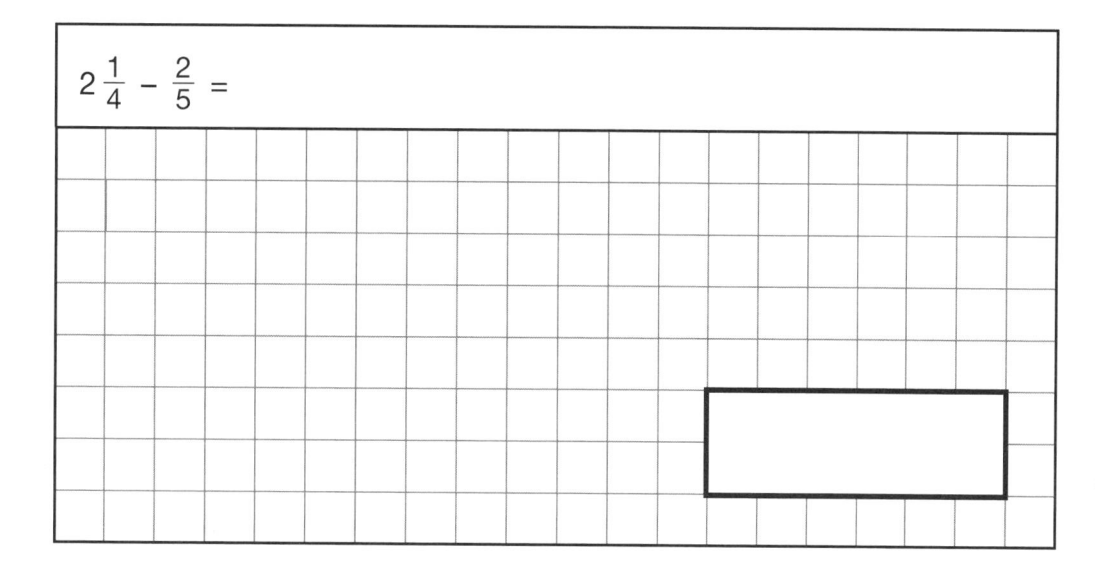

1 mark

5

$2\frac{1}{4} - \frac{2}{5} =$

1 mark

6 A, B and C are three corners of a rectangle.

Mark on the missing fourth corner (D) and then draw the rectangle.

Use a ruler.

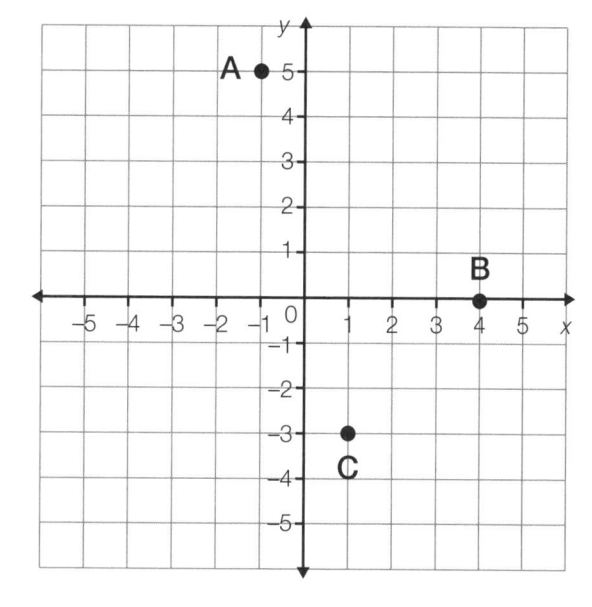

1 mark

What are the coordinates of D?

D = (,)

1 mark

Set B Test 11

7 Here are four labels.

(not multiples of 7)   (multiples of 3)   (multiples of 7)   (not multiples of 3)

Write each label in the correct position on the sorting diagram below.

	42 21	51 27
	28 70	26 17

1 mark

8 Zara's dad took up jogging to try to lose 28 pounds (lb) in weight.
This table shows how much weight he lost each fortnight for 20 weeks.

Week	0	2	4	6	8	10	12	14	16	18	20
Weight lost (lb)	0	2	3	2	2	3	1.5	2.5	1.5	1.5	1

Zara's dad did not achieve his goal.

Explain how you know.

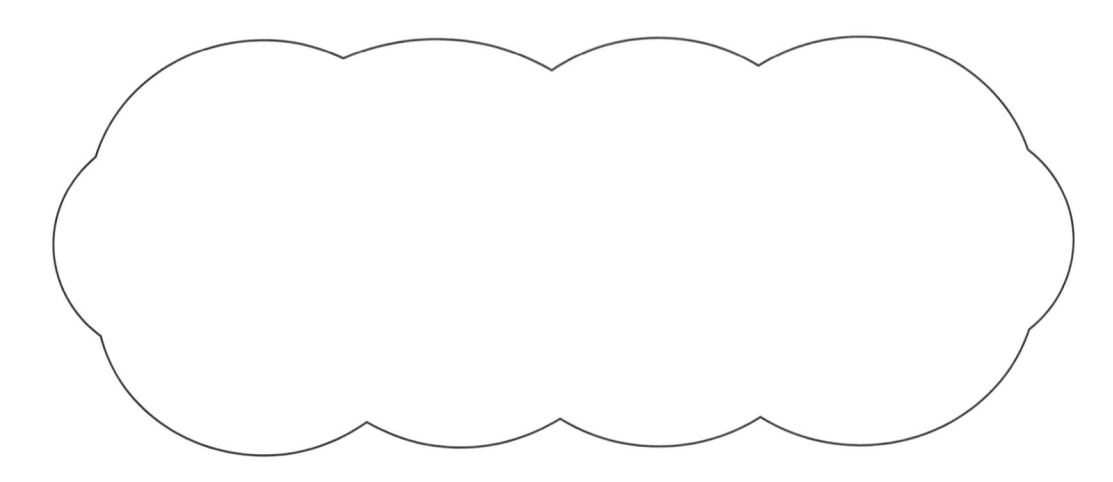

1 mark

During which week is it likely he was halfway to his goal?

Week [ ]

1 mark

[END OF TEST]

Set B Scoresheet

Scoresheet

When you finish the tests in Set B, write your marks in the boxes.

Test 1		/10
Test 2		/10
Test 3		/10
Test 4		/10
Test 5		/10
Test 6		/10
Test 7		/10
Test 8		/10
Test 9		/10
Test 10		/10
Test 11		/10
Total:		/110

How did you do?

0–59
Good start! Have another go at the questions in this book. Keep practising and you'll get there!

60–84
Well done! You're already doing well, but have another look at the topics you found difficult to make sure you're on track.

85–110
Fantastic! Give yourself a pat on the back. And remember you can improve even more by practising the things you find difficult.

A note for parents
Set B is designed to be equivalent to a full set of SATs tests. The exact number of marks students need in order to reach the expected standard in the real tests will vary from year to year. Based on previous assessments, we think students who score 60 or more in Set B are working at or above the expected standard.

Set A Answers

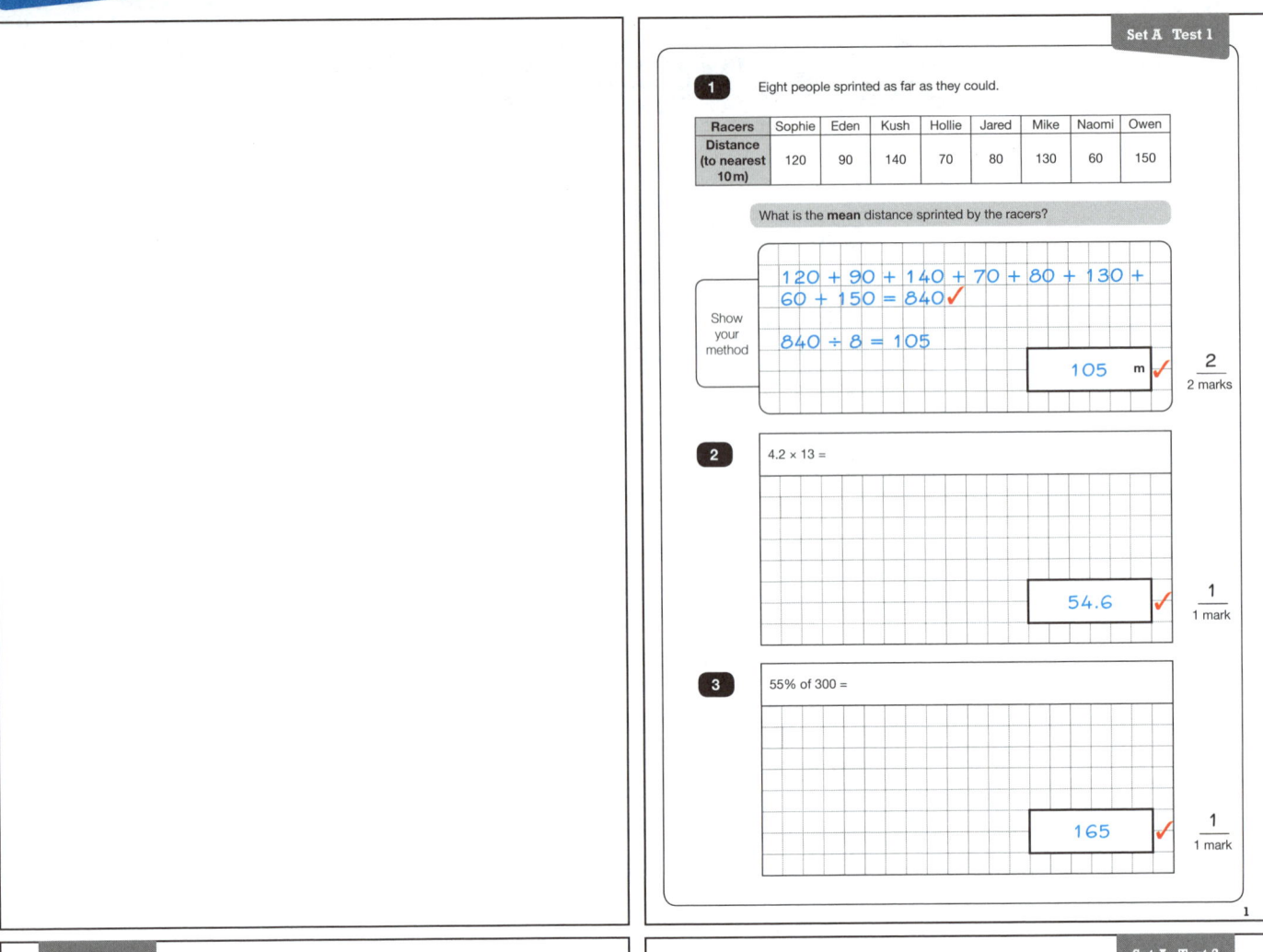

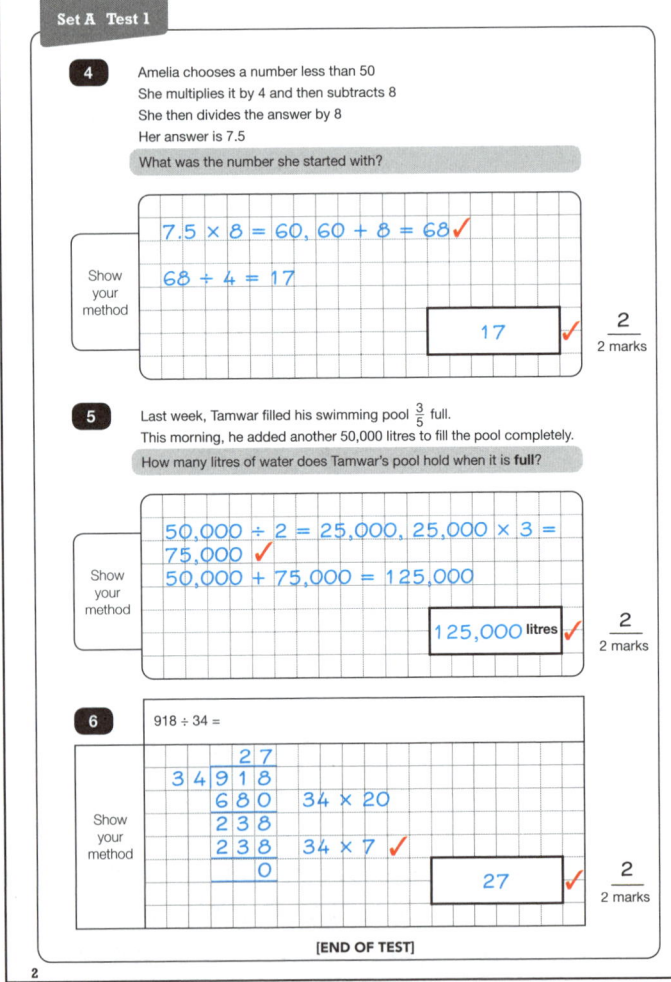

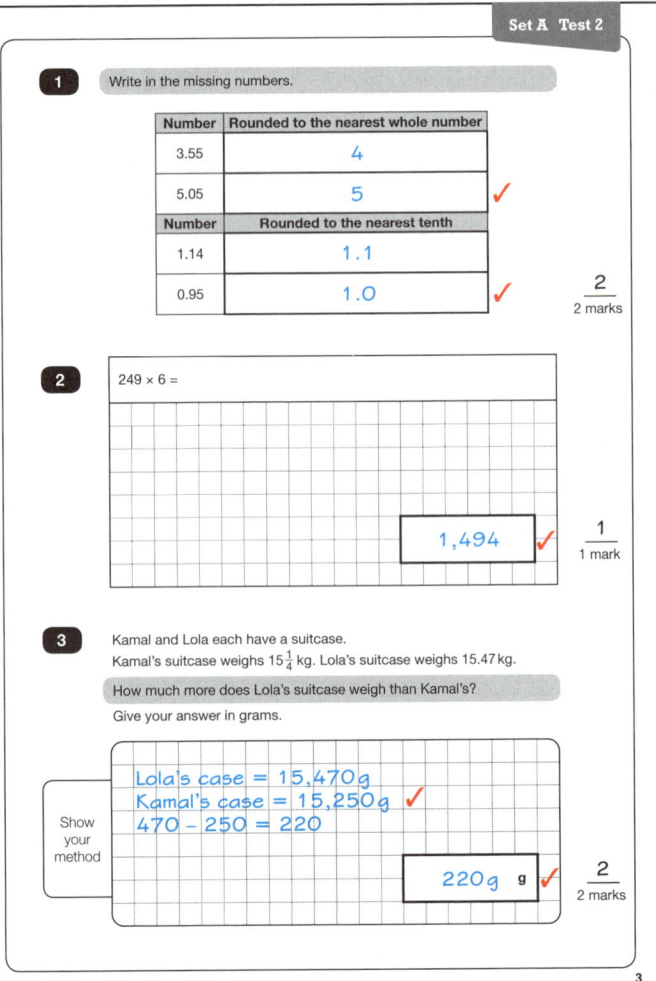

Set A Test 1

1 Eight people sprinted as far as they could.

Racers	Sophie	Eden	Kush	Hollie	Jared	Mike	Naomi	Owen
Distance (to nearest 10 m)	120	90	140	70	80	130	60	150

What is the **mean** distance sprinted by the racers?

Show your method:
120 + 90 + 140 + 70 + 80 + 130 + 60 + 150 = 840 ✓
840 ÷ 8 = 105

105 m ✓

2/2 marks

2 4.2 × 13 =

54.6 ✓

1/1 mark

3 55% of 300 =

165 ✓

1/1 mark

Set A Test 1 (continued)

4 Amelia chooses a number less than 50.
She multiplies it by 4 and then subtracts 8.
She then divides the answer by 8.
Her answer is 7.5.
What was the number she started with?

Show your method:
7.5 × 8 = 60, 60 + 8 = 68 ✓
68 ÷ 4 = 17

17 ✓

2/2 marks

5 Last week, Tamwar filled his swimming pool $\frac{3}{5}$ full.
This morning, he added another 50,000 litres to fill the pool completely.
How many litres of water does Tamwar's pool hold when it is **full**?

Show your method:
50,000 ÷ 2 = 25,000, 25,000 × 3 = 75,000 ✓
50,000 + 75,000 = 125,000

125,000 litres ✓

2/2 marks

6 918 ÷ 34 =

```
      2 7
3 4 ) 9 1 8
      6 8 0   34 × 20
      2 3 8
      2 3 8   34 × 7 ✓
          0
```

27 ✓

2/2 marks

[END OF TEST]

Set A Test 2

1 Write in the missing numbers.

Number	Rounded to the nearest whole number
3.55	4
5.05	5 ✓

Number	Rounded to the nearest tenth
1.14	1.1
0.95	1.0 ✓

2/2 marks

2 249 × 6 =

1,494 ✓

1/1 mark

3 Kamal and Lola each have a suitcase.
Kamal's suitcase weighs $15\frac{1}{4}$ kg. Lola's suitcase weighs 15.47 kg.
How much more does Lola's suitcase weigh than Kamal's?
Give your answer in grams.

Show your method:
Lola's case = 15,470 g
Kamal's case = 15,250 g ✓
470 − 250 = 220

220 g ✓

2/2 marks

62

Set A Answers

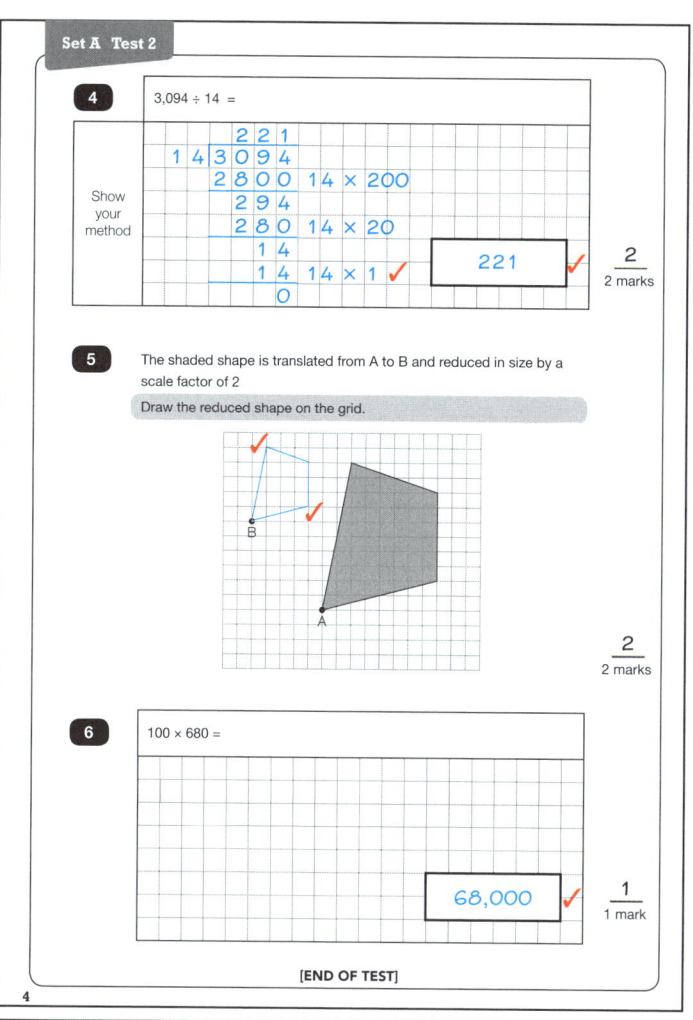

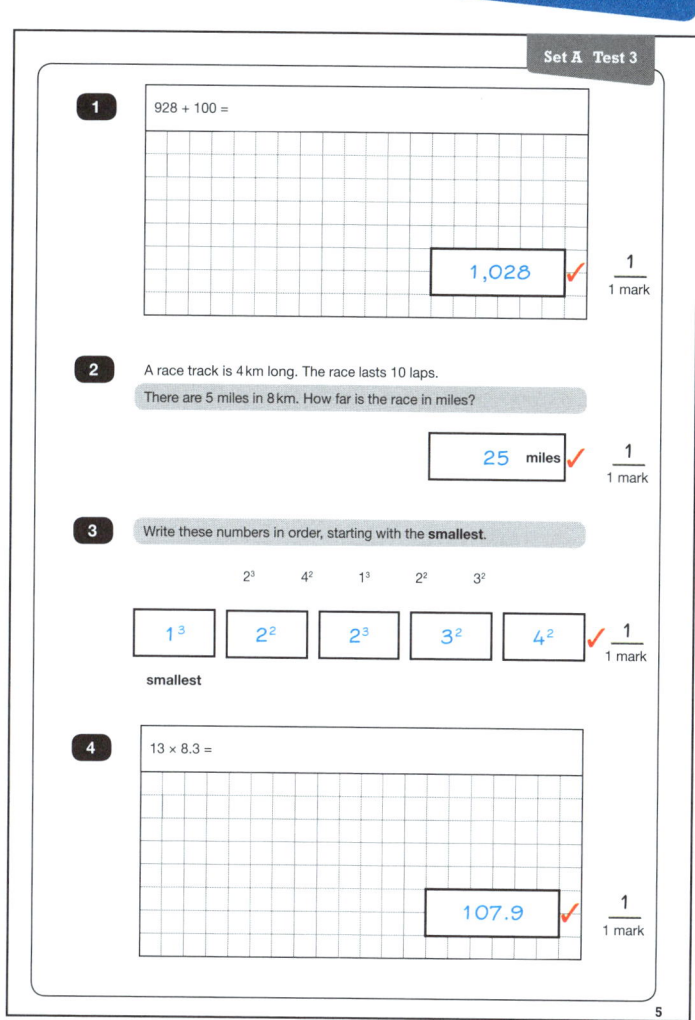

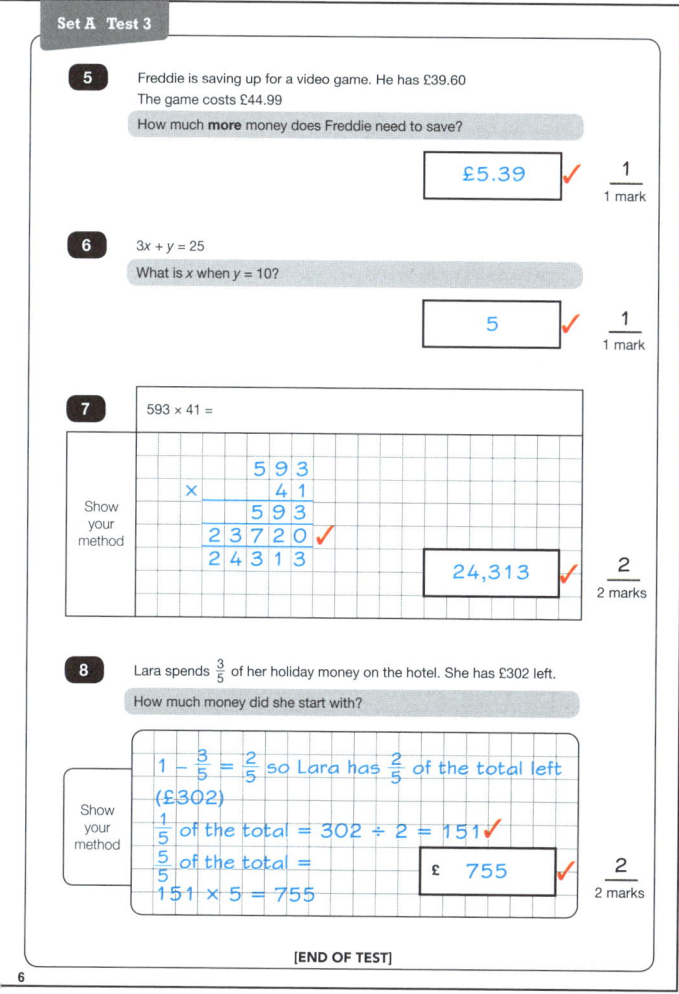

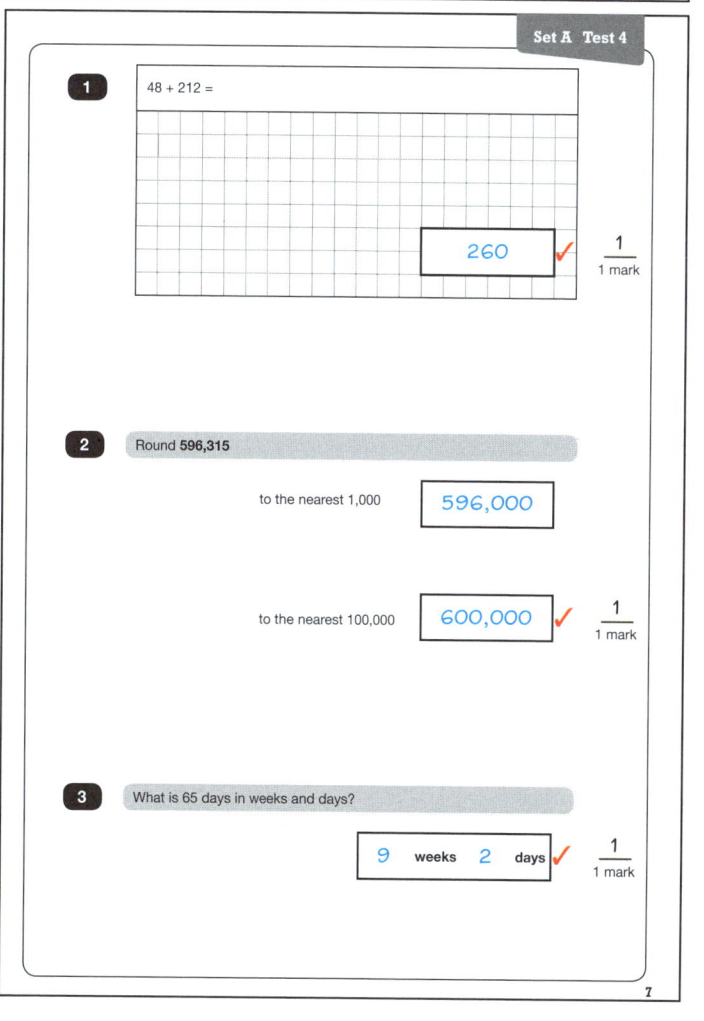

Set A Test 2

4 $3{,}094 \div 14 =$

Show your method:
```
      2 2 1
1 4 ) 3 0 9 4
      2 8 0 0    14 × 200
        2 9 4
        2 8 0    14 × 20
          1 4
          1 4    14 × 1 ✓
           0
```
221 ✓ — 2/2 marks

5 The shaded shape is translated from A to B and reduced in size by a scale factor of 2.

Draw the reduced shape on the grid. — 2/2 marks

6 $100 \times 680 =$ **68,000** ✓ — 1/1 mark

[END OF TEST]

Set A Test 3

1 $928 + 100 =$ **1,028** ✓ — 1/1 mark

2 A race track is 4 km long. The race lasts 10 laps.
There are 5 miles in 8 km. How far is the race in miles?
25 miles ✓ — 1/1 mark

3 Write these numbers in order, starting with the **smallest**.

$2^3 \quad 4^2 \quad 1^3 \quad 2^2 \quad 3^2$

| 1^3 | 2^2 | 2^3 | 3^2 | 4^2 |

smallest — 1/1 mark

4 $13 \times 8.3 =$ **107.9** ✓ — 1/1 mark

Set A Test 3 (continued)

5 Freddie is saving up for a video game. He has £39.60
The game costs £44.99
How much **more** money does Freddie need to save?
£5.39 ✓ — 1/1 mark

6 $3x + y = 25$
What is x when $y = 10$?
5 ✓ — 1/1 mark

7 $593 \times 41 =$

Show your method:
```
        5 9 3
    ×     4 1
        5 9 3
    2 3 7 2 0 ✓
    2 4 3 1 3
```
24,313 ✓ — 2/2 marks

8 Lara spends $\frac{3}{5}$ of her holiday money on the hotel. She has £302 left.
How much money did she start with?

Show your method:
$1 - \frac{3}{5} = \frac{2}{5}$ so Lara has $\frac{2}{5}$ of the total left (£302)
$\frac{1}{5}$ of the total $= 302 \div 2 = 151$ ✓
$\frac{5}{5}$ of the total $= 151 \times 5 = 755$

£755 ✓ — 2/2 marks

[END OF TEST]

Set A Test 4

1 $48 + 212 =$ **260** ✓ — 1/1 mark

2 Round **596,315**

to the nearest 1,000 — **596,000** ✓
to the nearest 100,000 — **600,000** ✓ — 1/1 mark

3 What is 65 days in weeks and days?
9 weeks **2** days ✓ — 1/1 mark

63

Set A Answers

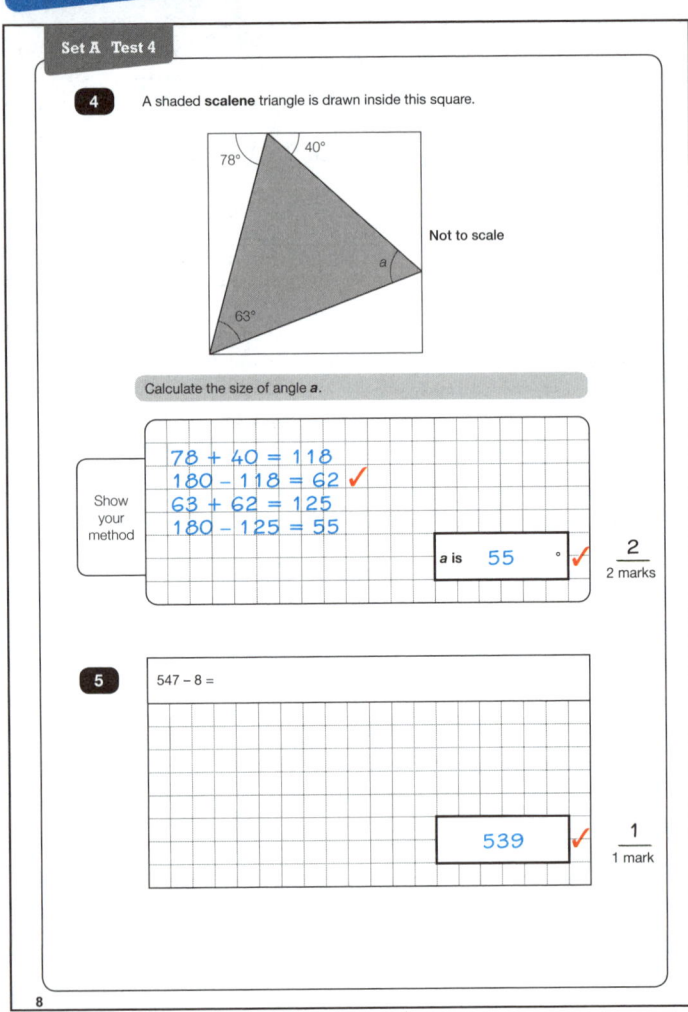

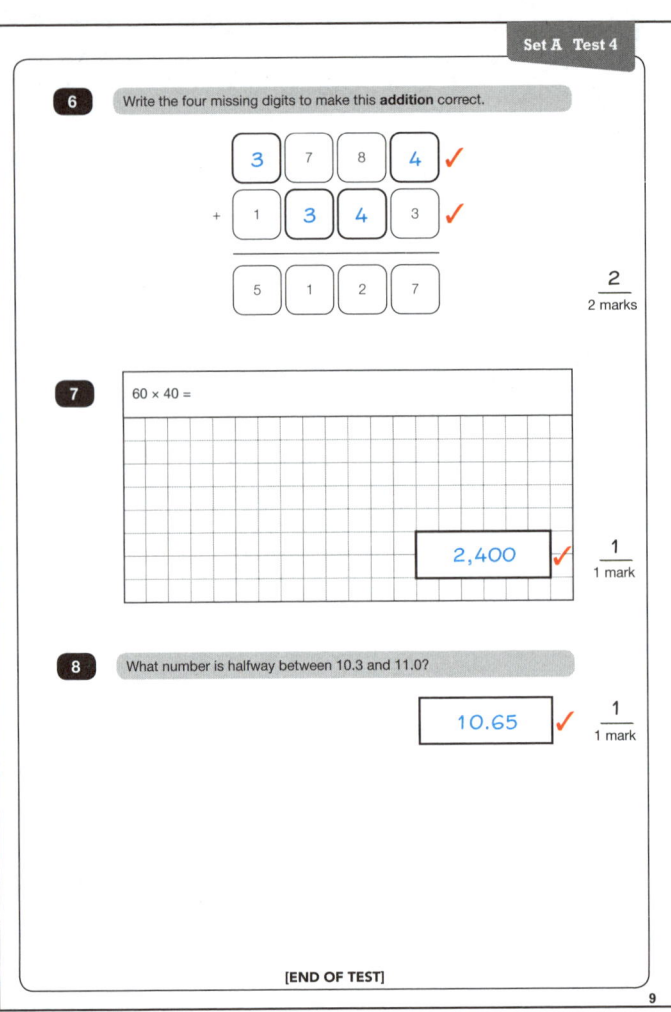

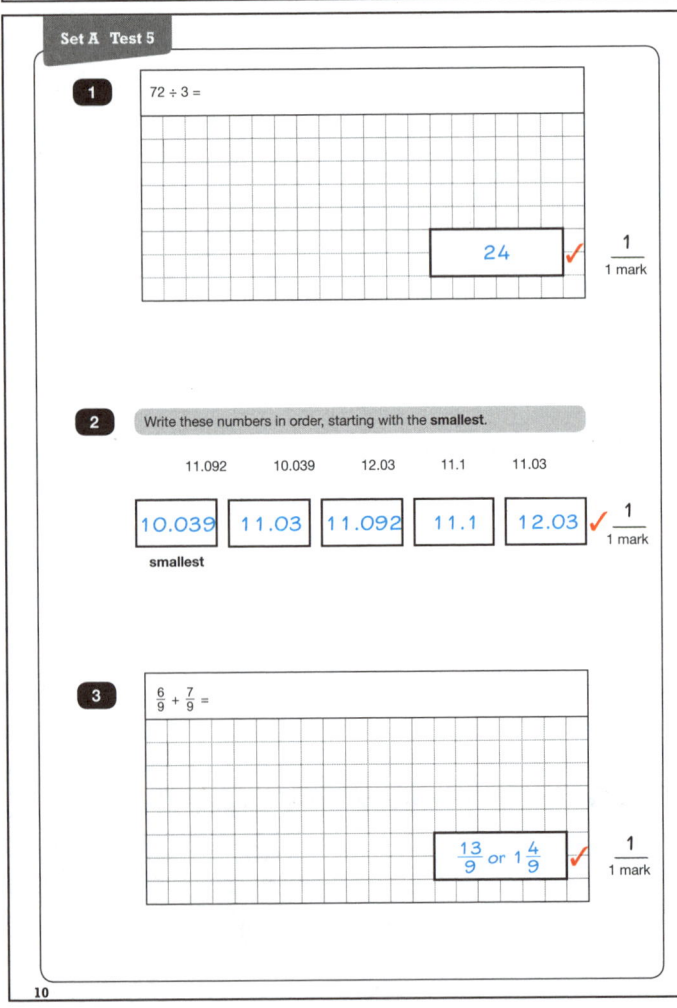

Set A Test 4

4. A shaded **scalene** triangle is drawn inside this square.

78°, 40°, 63°, Not to scale

Calculate the size of angle *a*.

Show your method:
78 + 40 = 118
180 − 118 = 62 ✓
63 + 62 = 125
180 − 125 = 55

a is **55** ° ✓

2 / 2 marks

5. 547 − 8 = **539** ✓

1 / 1 mark

6. Write the four missing digits to make this **addition** correct.

```
  3  7  8  4  ✓
+ 1  3  4  3  ✓
-------------
  5  1  2  7
```

2 / 2 marks

7. 60 × 40 = **2,400** ✓

1 / 1 mark

8. What number is halfway between 10.3 and 11.0?

10.65 ✓

1 / 1 mark

[END OF TEST]

Set A Test 5

1. 72 ÷ 3 = **24** ✓

1 / 1 mark

2. Write these numbers in order, starting with the **smallest**.

11.092   10.039   12.03   11.1   11.03

10.039 | **11.03** | **11.092** | **11.1** | **12.03** ✓
smallest

1 / 1 mark

3. $\frac{6}{9} + \frac{7}{9} =$ **$\frac{13}{9}$ or $1\frac{4}{9}$** ✓

1 / 1 mark

4. This 3D shape is called an icosahedron. Some of its faces are shaded.

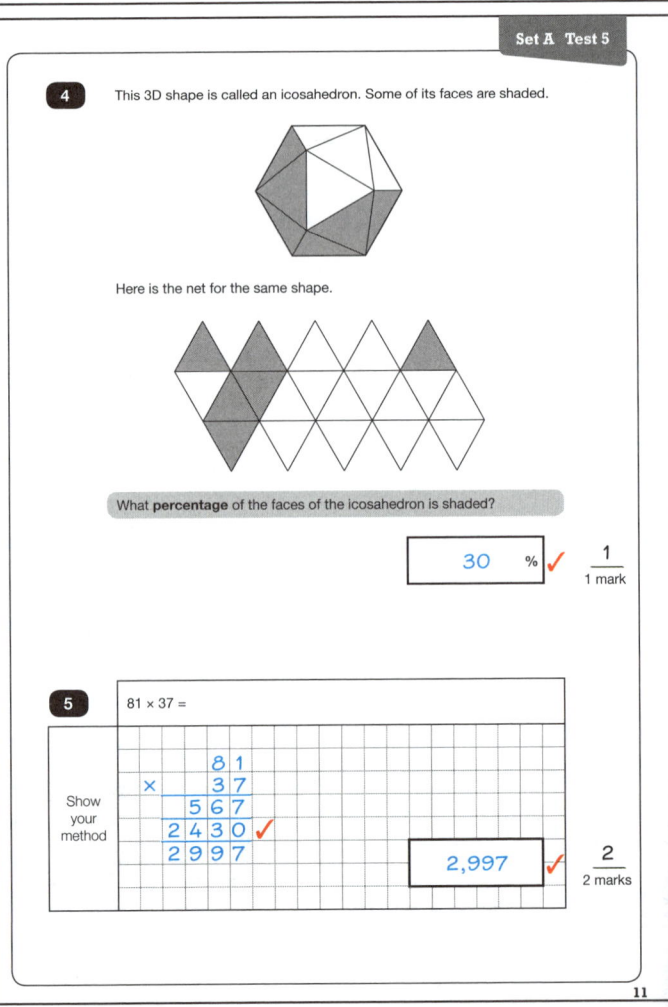

Here is the net for the same shape.

What **percentage** of the faces of the icosahedron is shaded?

30 % ✓

1 / 1 mark

5. 81 × 37 =

Show your method:
```
      8 1
   ×  3 7
   -----
    5 6 7
  2 4 3 0  ✓
  -------
  2 9 9 7
```

2,997 ✓

2 / 2 marks

Set A Answers

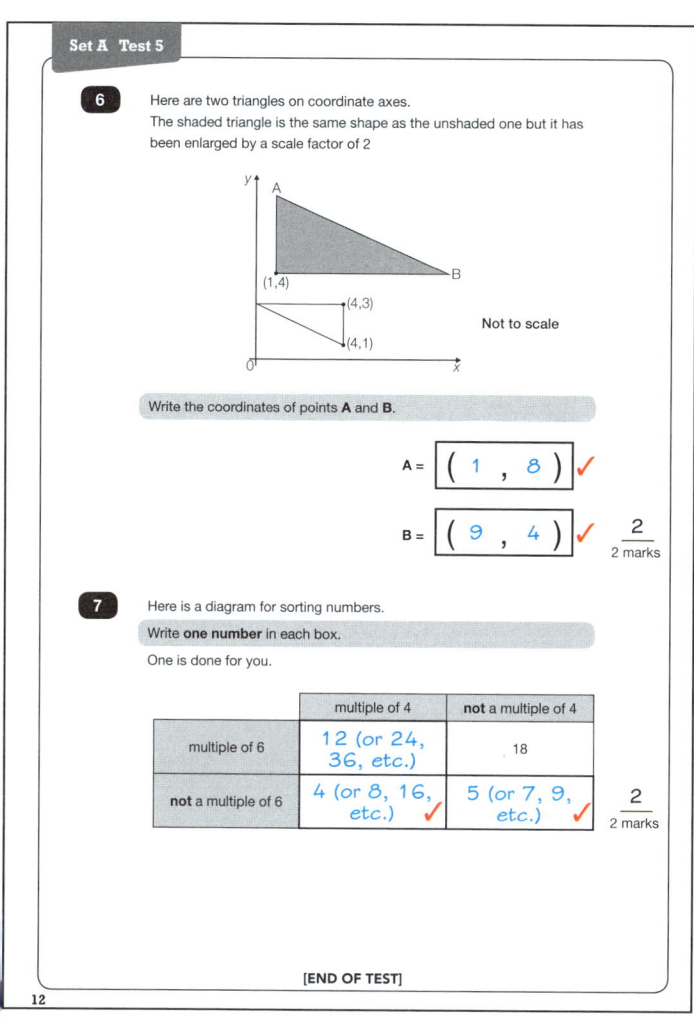

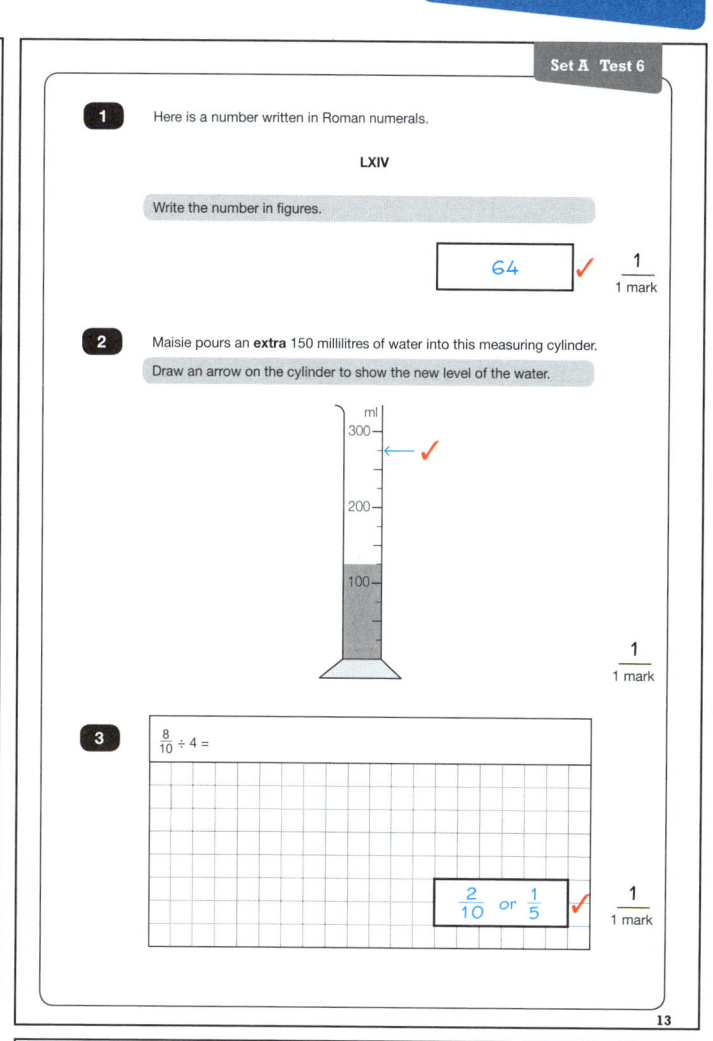

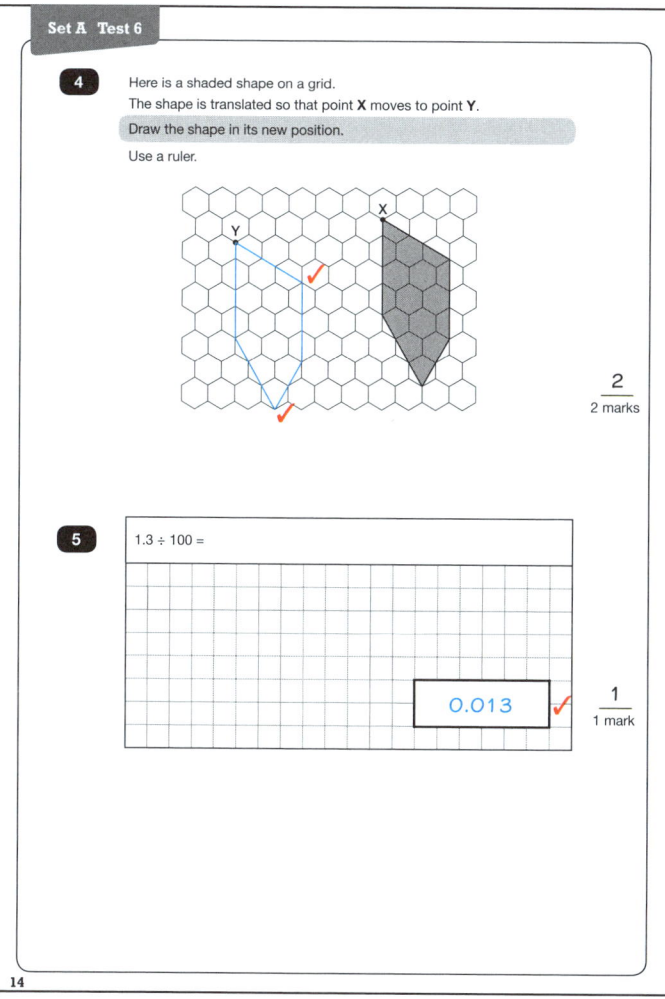

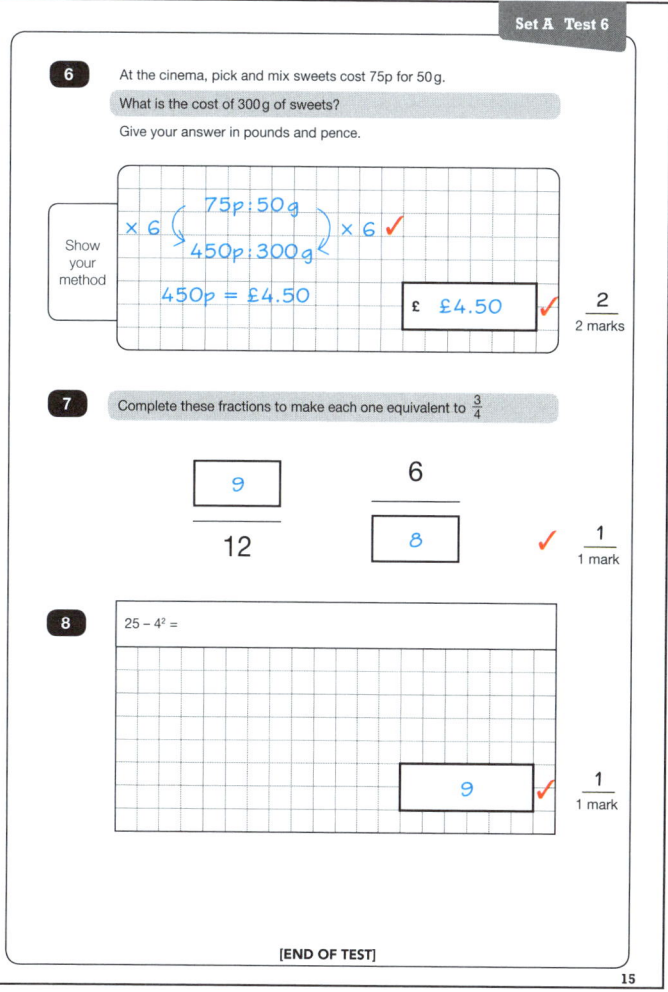

Set A Test 5

6 Here are two triangles on coordinate axes.
The shaded triangle is the same shape as the unshaded one but it has been enlarged by a scale factor of 2

Not to scale

Write the coordinates of points **A** and **B**.

A = (1 , 8) ✓

B = (9 , 4) ✓

2 / 2 marks

7 Here is a diagram for sorting numbers.
Write **one number** in each box.
One is done for you.

	multiple of 4	**not** a multiple of 4
multiple of 6	12 (or 24, 36, etc.)	18
not a multiple of 6	4 (or 8, 16, etc.) ✓	5 (or 7, 9, etc.) ✓

2 / 2 marks

[END OF TEST]

Set A Test 6

1 Here is a number written in Roman numerals.

LXIV

Write the number in figures.

64 ✓

1 / 1 mark

2 Maisie pours an **extra** 150 millilitres of water into this measuring cylinder.
Draw an arrow on the cylinder to show the new level of the water.

✓

1 / 1 mark

3 $\frac{8}{10} \div 4 =$

$\frac{2}{10}$ or $\frac{1}{5}$ ✓

1 / 1 mark

Set A Test 6

4 Here is a shaded shape on a grid.
The shape is translated so that point **X** moves to point **Y**.
Draw the shape in its new position.
Use a ruler.

✓

2 / 2 marks

5 $1.3 \div 100 =$

0.013 ✓

1 / 1 mark

Set A Test 6

6 At the cinema, pick and mix sweets cost 75p for 50g.
What is the cost of 300g of sweets?
Give your answer in pounds and pence.

Show your method:
75p : 50g
×6 (450p : 300g) ×6 ✓
450p = £4.50

£ £4.50 ✓

2 / 2 marks

7 Complete these fractions to make each one equivalent to $\frac{3}{4}$

$\frac{9}{12}$ $\frac{6}{8}$ ✓

1 / 1 mark

8 $25 - 4^2 =$

9 ✓

1 / 1 mark

[END OF TEST]

65

Set A Answers

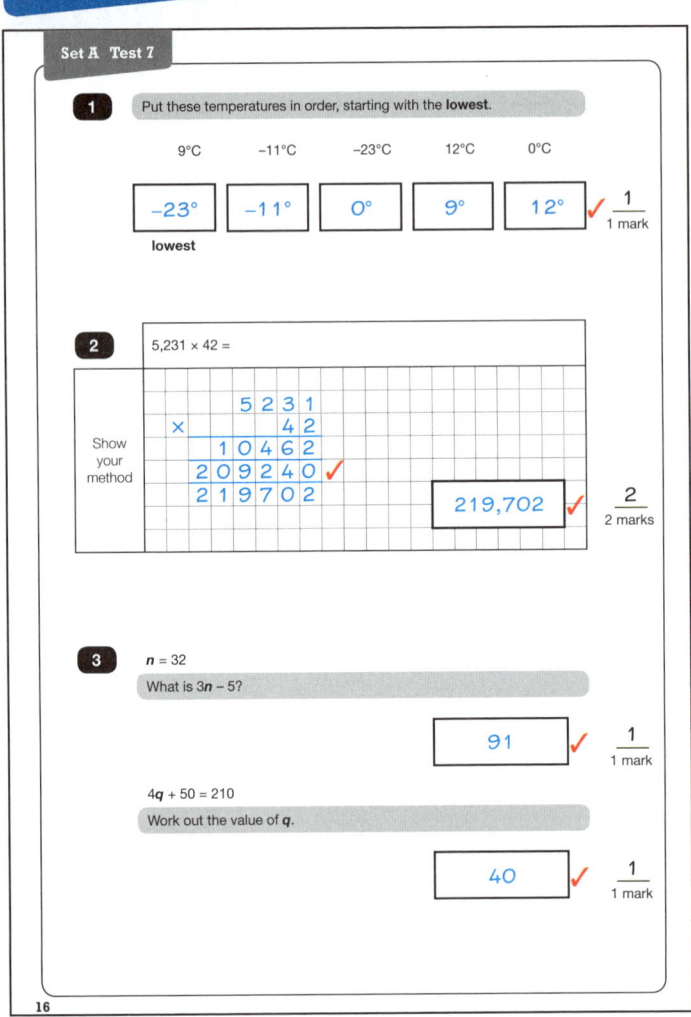

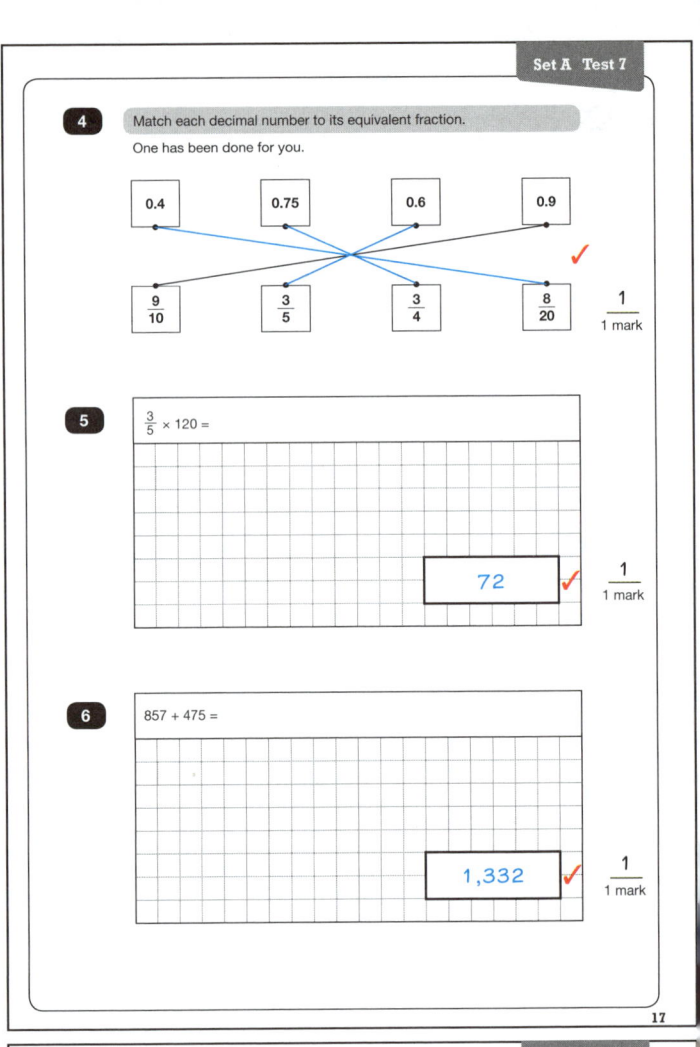

Set A Test 7

1 Put these temperatures in order, starting with the **lowest**.

9°C   −11°C   −23°C   12°C   0°C

−23°	−11°	0°	9°	12°	✓
lowest					

1 / 1 mark

2 5,231 × 42 =

Show your method:
```
      5 2 3 1
  ×       4 2
  1 0 4 6 2
2 0 9 2 4 0 ✓
2 1 9 7 0 2
```

219,702 ✓

2 / 2 marks

3 $n = 32$

What is $3n - 5$?

91 ✓

1 / 1 mark

$4q + 50 = 210$

Work out the value of q.

40 ✓

1 / 1 mark

Set A Test 7

4 Match each decimal number to its equivalent fraction.
One has been done for you.

0.4 — $\frac{8}{20}$
0.75 — $\frac{3}{4}$
0.6 — $\frac{3}{5}$
0.9 — $\frac{9}{10}$ ✓

1 / 1 mark

5 $\frac{3}{5} \times 120 =$

72 ✓

1 / 1 mark

6 $857 + 475 =$

1,332 ✓

1 / 1 mark

Set A Test 7

7 Look at this 3D shape.
(4 cm × 2 cm × 2 cm cuboid)

Draw two more faces on this centimetre dotted paper to complete the net of this shape.
Use a ruler.

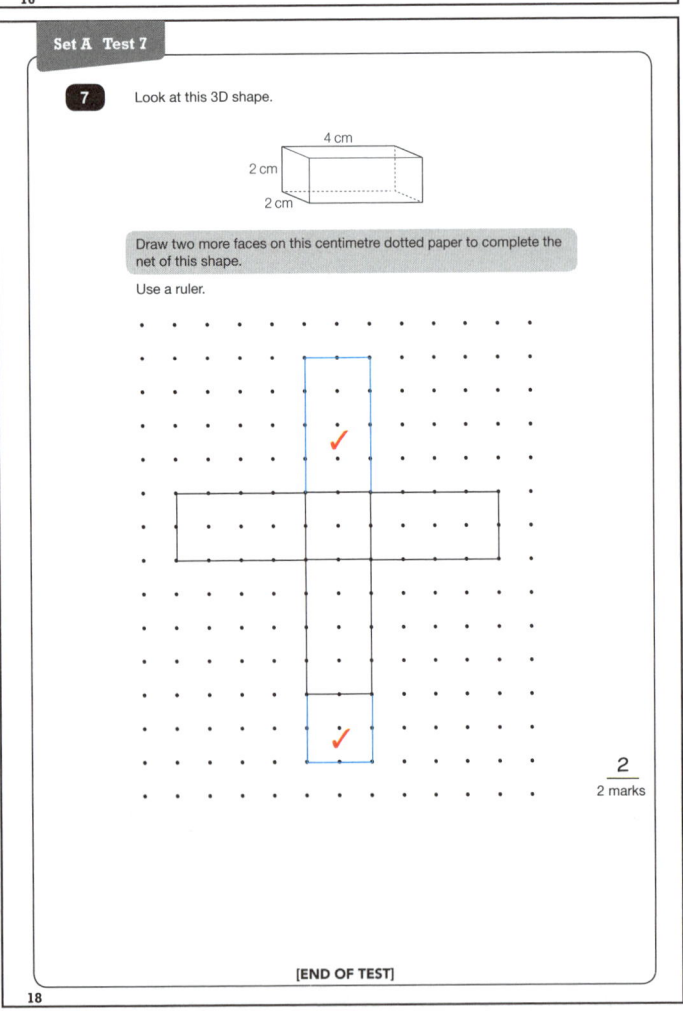

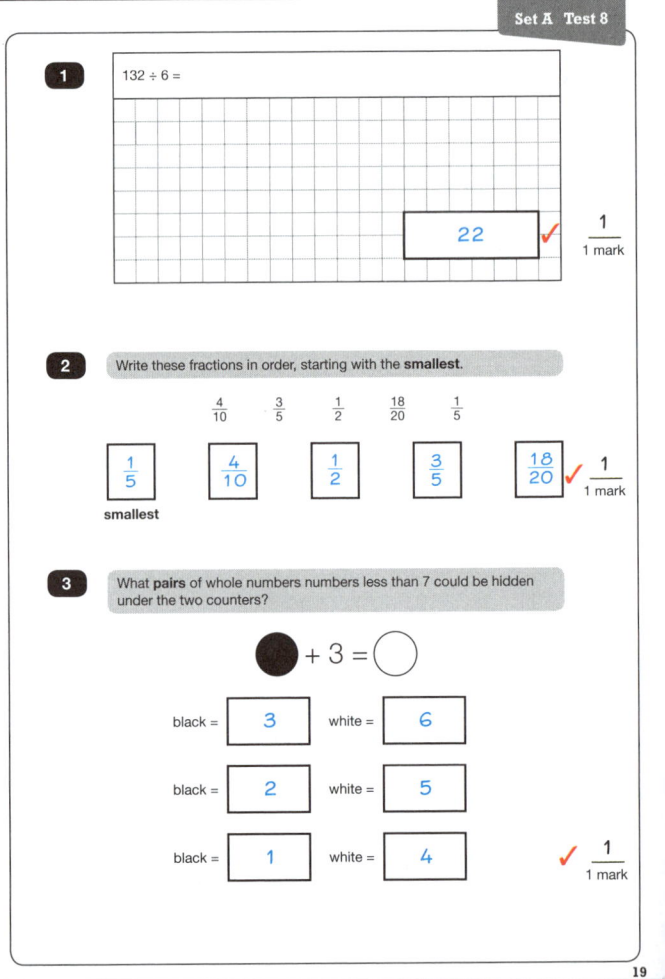

✓ ✓

2 / 2 marks

[END OF TEST]

Set A Test 8

1 $132 \div 6 =$

22 ✓

1 / 1 mark

2 Write these fractions in order, starting with the **smallest**.

$\frac{4}{10}$ $\frac{3}{5}$ $\frac{1}{2}$ $\frac{18}{20}$ $\frac{1}{5}$

$\frac{1}{5}$	$\frac{4}{10}$	$\frac{1}{2}$	$\frac{3}{5}$	$\frac{18}{20}$ ✓
smallest				

1 / 1 mark

3 What **pairs** of whole numbers less than 7 could be hidden under the two counters?

● + 3 = ○

black = 3   white = 6

black = 2   white = 5

black = 1   white = 4 ✓

1 / 1 mark

Set A Answers

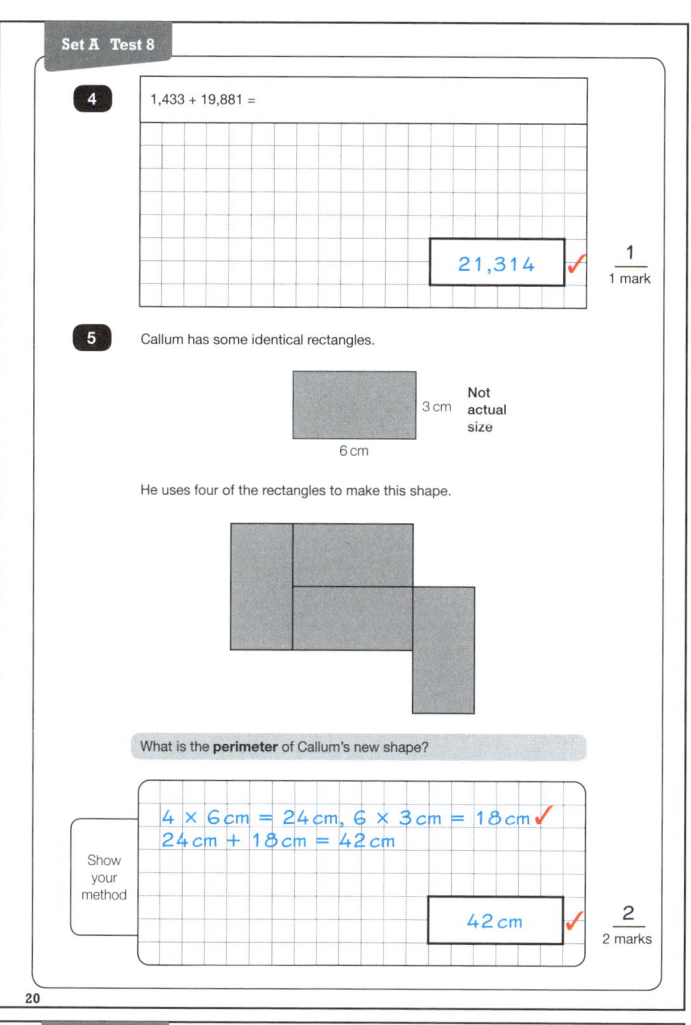

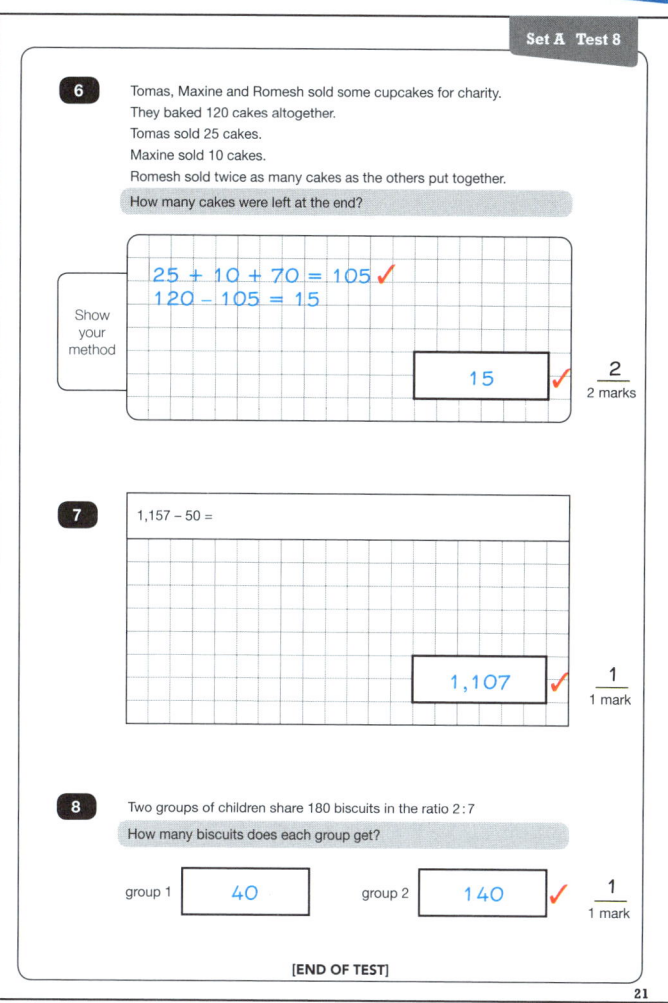

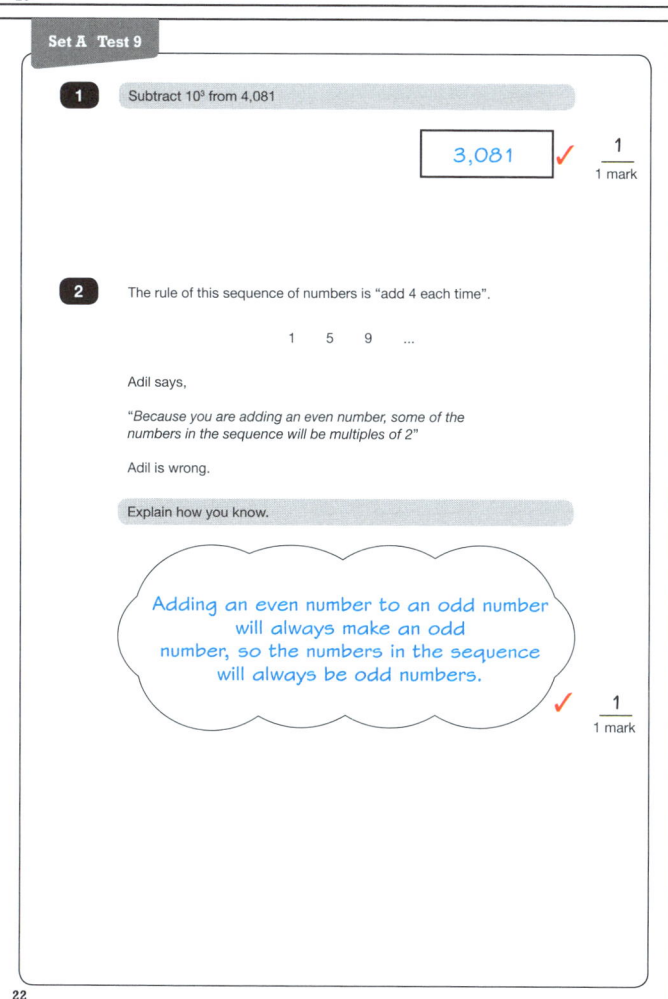

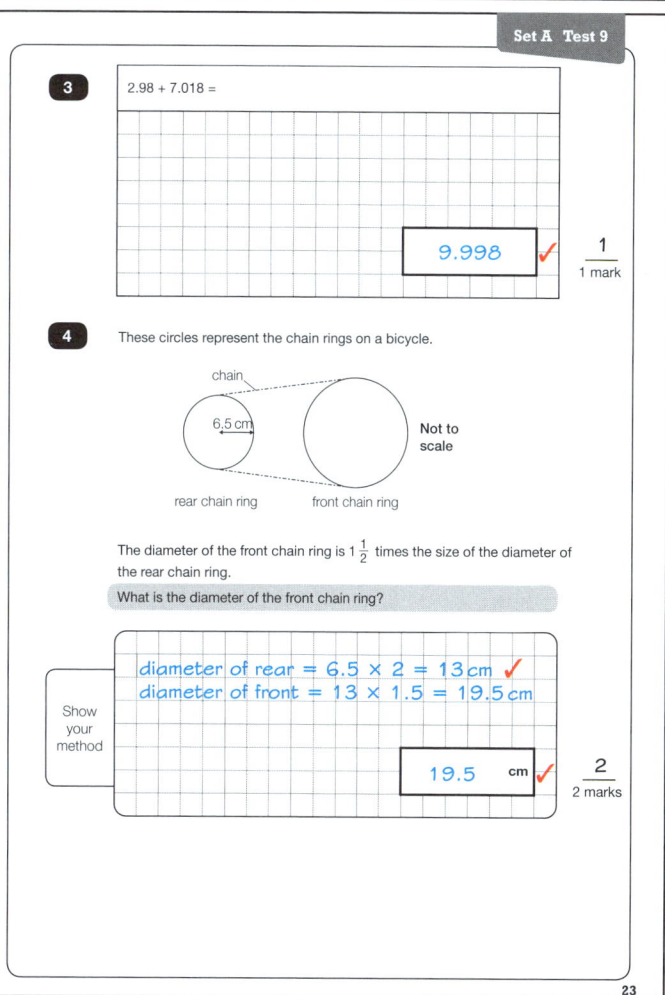

Set A Test 8

4 1,433 + 19,881 =

21,314 ✓ — 1/1 mark

5 Callum has some identical rectangles.

3 cm, 6 cm — Not actual size

He uses four of the rectangles to make this shape.

What is the **perimeter** of Callum's new shape?

Show your method:
4 × 6 cm = 24 cm, 6 × 3 cm = 18 cm ✓
24 cm + 18 cm = 42 cm

42 cm ✓ — 2/2 marks

6 Tomas, Maxine and Romesh sold some cupcakes for charity.
They baked 120 cakes altogether.
Tomas sold 25 cakes.
Maxine sold 10 cakes.
Romesh sold twice as many cakes as the others put together.
How many cakes were left at the end?

Show your method:
25 + 10 + 70 = 105 ✓
120 − 105 = 15

15 ✓ — 2/2 marks

7 1,157 − 50 =

1,107 ✓ — 1/1 mark

8 Two groups of children share 180 biscuits in the ratio 2:7
How many biscuits does each group get?

group 1 **40**   group 2 **140** ✓ — 1/1 mark

[END OF TEST]

Set A Test 9

1 Subtract 10^3 from 4,081

3,081 ✓ — 1/1 mark

2 The rule of this sequence of numbers is "add 4 each time".

1   5   9   ...

Adil says,

"Because you are adding an even number, some of the numbers in the sequence will be multiples of 2"

Adil is wrong.

Explain how you know.

Adding an even number to an odd number will always make an odd number, so the numbers in the sequence will always be odd numbers. ✓ — 1/1 mark

3 2.98 + 7.018 =

9.998 ✓ — 1/1 mark

4 These circles represent the chain rings on a bicycle.

6.5 cm — rear chain ring, front chain ring — Not to scale

The diameter of the front chain ring is $1\frac{1}{2}$ times the size of the diameter of the rear chain ring.
What is the diameter of the front chain ring?

Show your method:
diameter of rear = 6.5 × 2 = 13 cm ✓
diameter of front = 13 × 1.5 = 19.5 cm

19.5 cm ✓ — 2/2 marks

Set A Answers

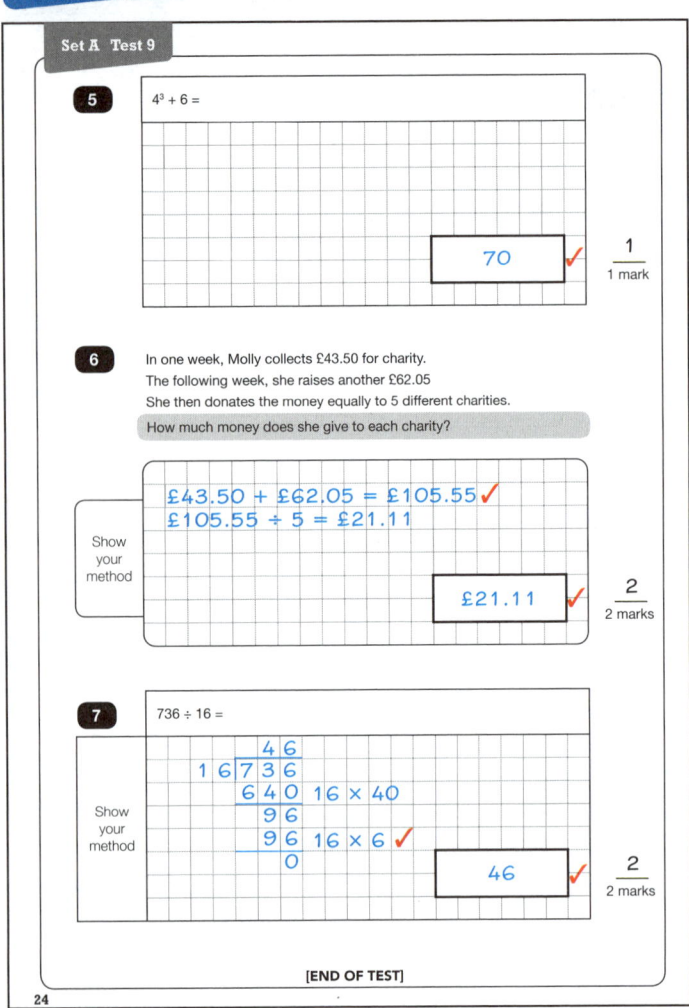

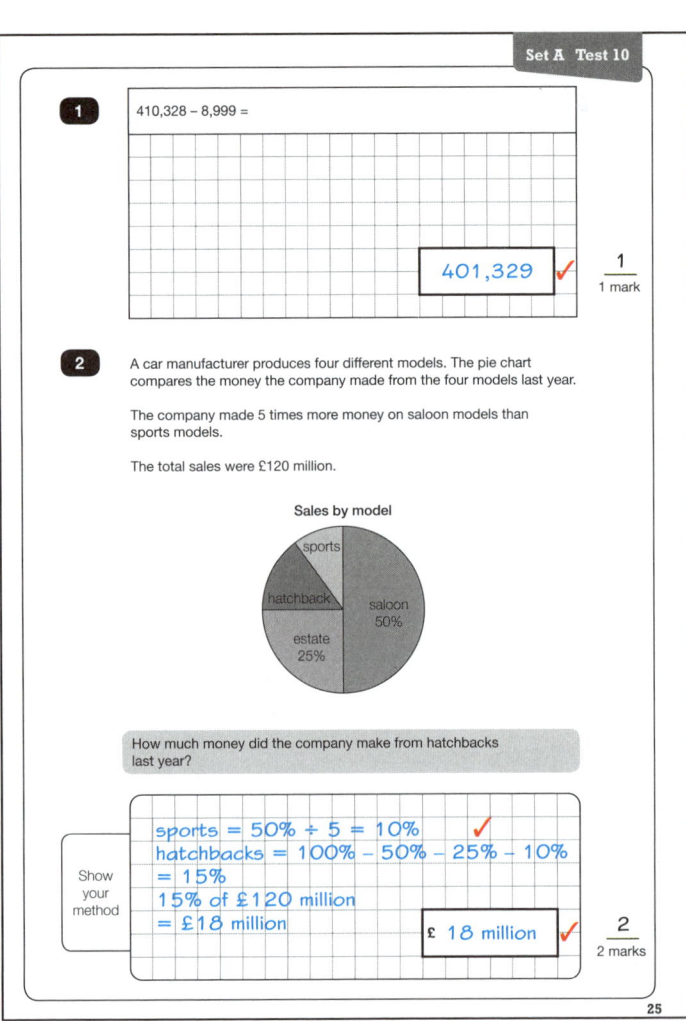

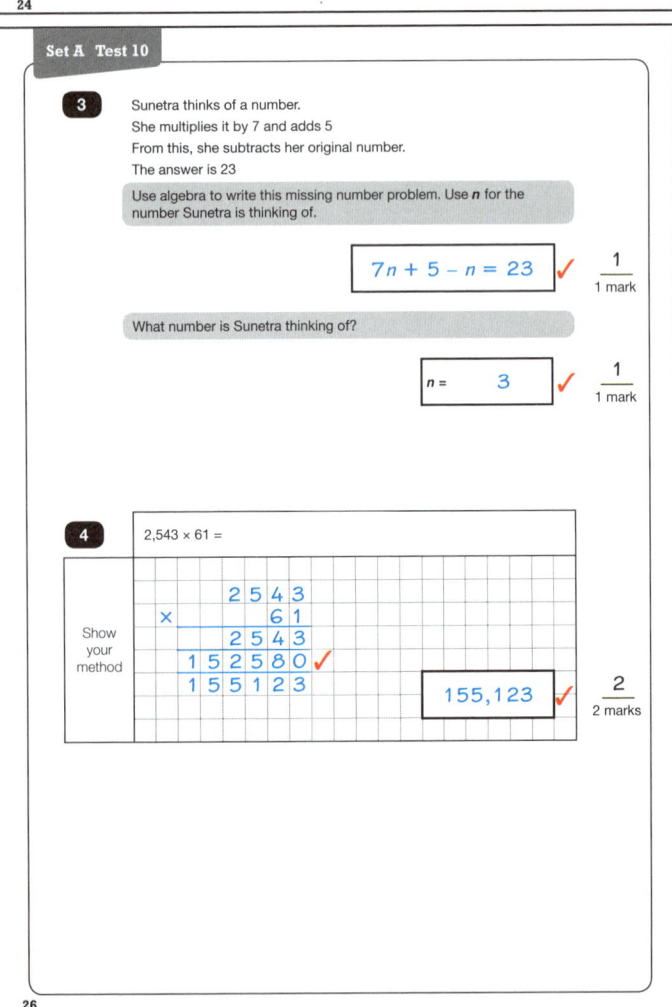

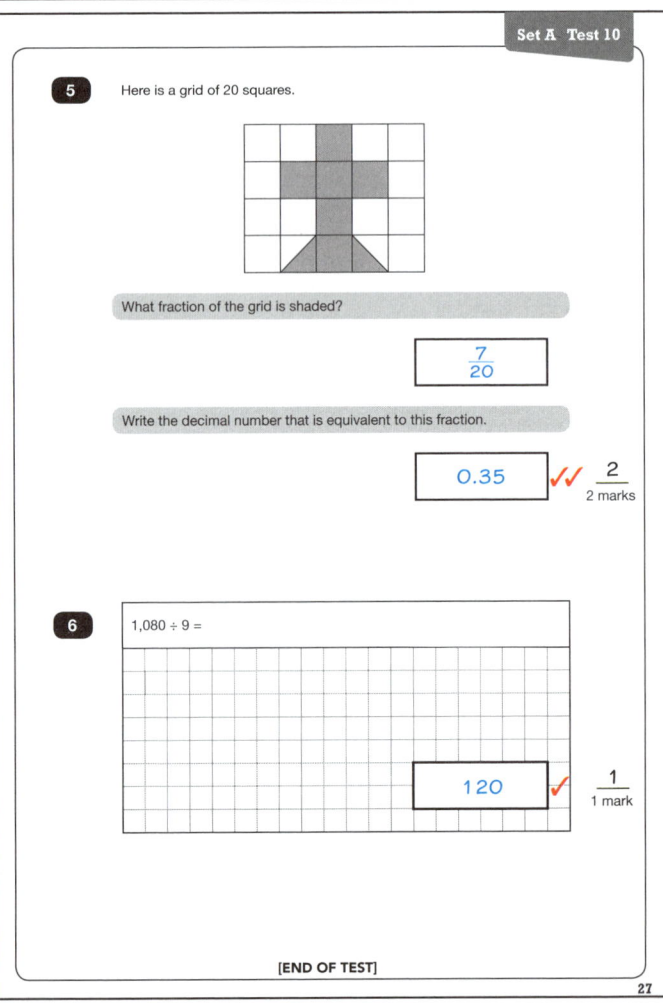

Set A Test 9

5 $4^3 + 6 =$

Answer: **70** ✓ — 1/1 mark

6 In one week, Molly collects £43.50 for charity.
The following week, she raises another £62.05
She then donates the money equally to 5 different charities.

How much money does she give to each charity?

Show your method:
£43.50 + £62.05 = £105.55 ✓
£105.55 ÷ 5 = £21.11

Answer: **£21.11** ✓ — 2/2 marks

7 $736 ÷ 16 =$

Show your method:
```
     4 6
16)7 3 6
   6 4 0   16 × 40
     9 6
     9 6   16 × 6 ✓
         0
```

Answer: **46** ✓ — 2/2 marks

[END OF TEST]

Set A Test 10

1 $410{,}328 - 8{,}999 =$

Answer: **401,329** ✓ — 1/1 mark

2 A car manufacturer produces four different models. The pie chart compares the money the company made from the four models last year.

The company made 5 times more money on saloon models than sports models.

The total sales were £120 million.

Sales by model (pie chart): sports, hatchback, estate 25%, saloon 50%

How much money did the company make from hatchbacks last year?

Show your method:
sports = 50% ÷ 5 = 10% ✓
hatchbacks = 100% − 50% − 25% − 10%
= 15%
15% of £120 million
= £18 million

Answer: **£18 million** ✓ — 2/2 marks

Set A Test 10

3 Sunetra thinks of a number.
She multiplies it by 7 and adds 5
From this, she subtracts her original number.
The answer is 23

Use algebra to write this missing number problem. Use n for the number Sunetra is thinking of.

Answer: **$7n + 5 - n = 23$** ✓ — 1/1 mark

What number is Sunetra thinking of?

Answer: **$n = 3$** ✓ — 1/1 mark

4 $2{,}543 × 61 =$

Show your method:
```
       2 5 4 3
    ×      6 1
       2 5 4 3
   1 5 2 5 8 0 ✓
   1 5 5 1 2 3
```

Answer: **155,123** ✓ — 2/2 marks

Set A Test 10

5 Here is a grid of 20 squares.

What fraction of the grid is shaded?

Answer: **$\frac{7}{20}$**

Write the decimal number that is equivalent to this fraction.

Answer: **0.35** ✓✓ — 2/2 marks

6 $1{,}080 ÷ 9 =$

Answer: **120** ✓ — 1/1 mark

[END OF TEST]

Set A Answers

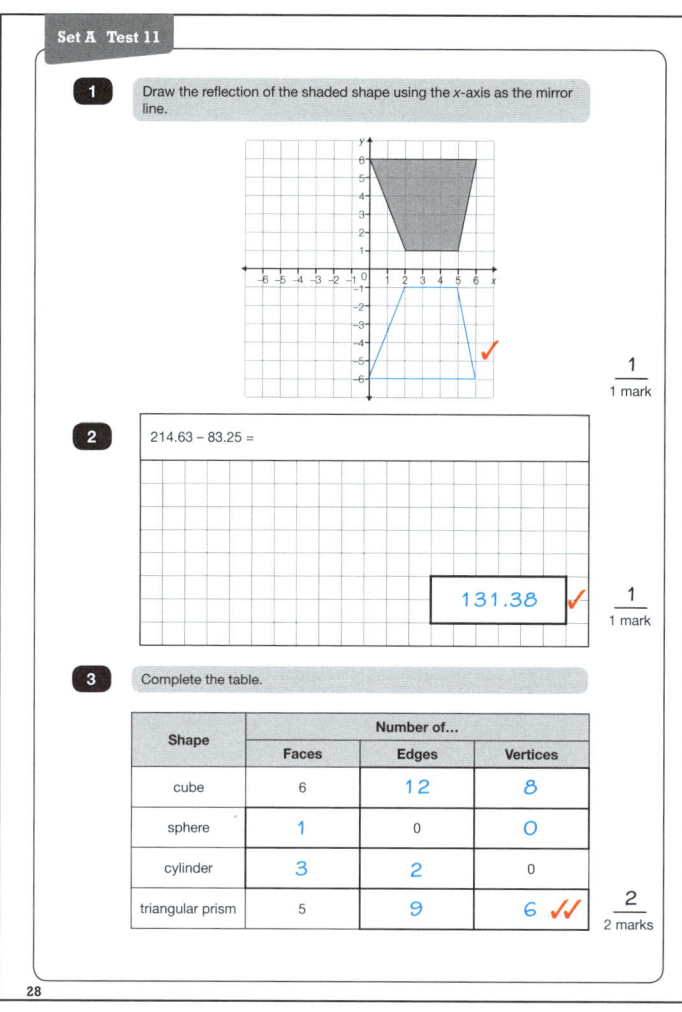

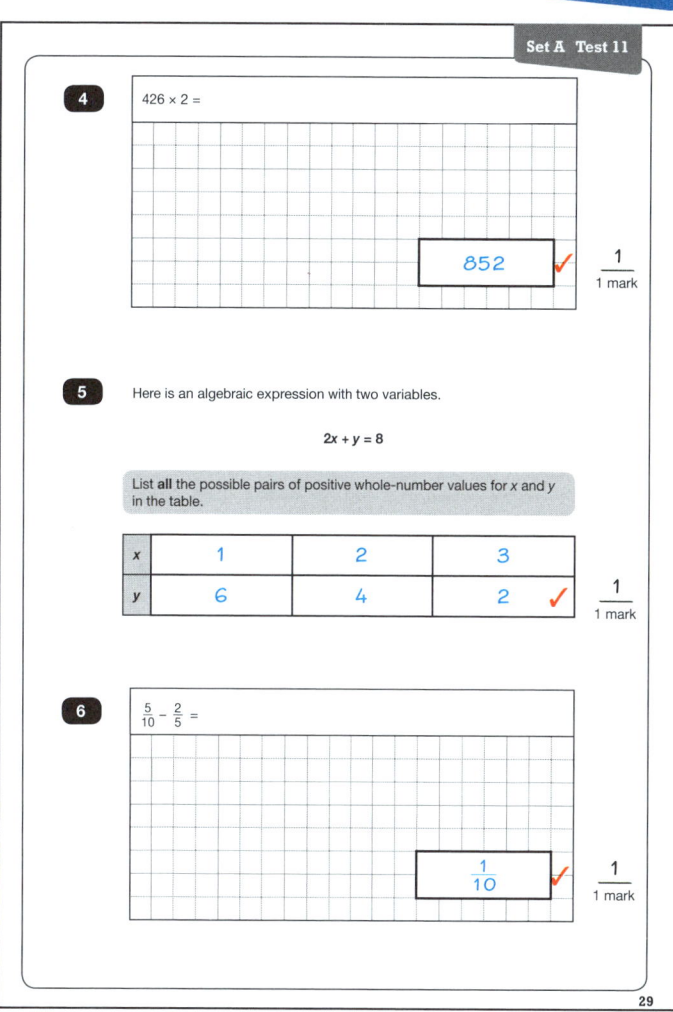

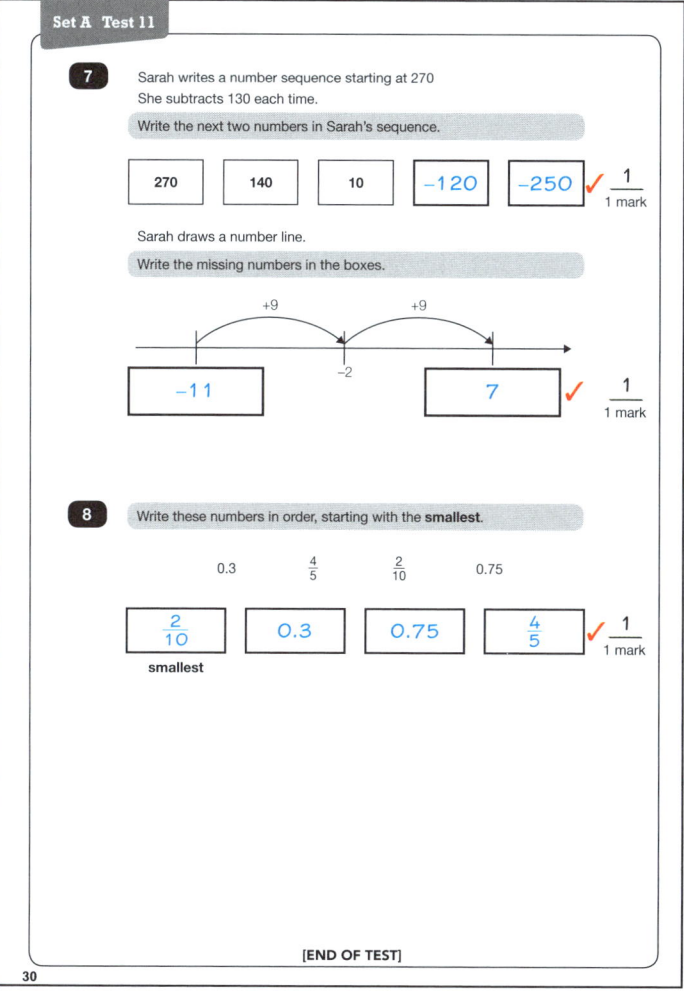

Set A Test 11

1 Draw the reflection of the shaded shape using the *x*-axis as the mirror line.

(Reflection drawn below x-axis) — 1/1 mark

2 214.63 − 83.25 =

131.38 ✓ — 1/1 mark

3 Complete the table.

Shape	Number of...		
	Faces	Edges	Vertices
cube	6	**12**	**8**
sphere	**1**	0	**0**
cylinder	**3**	**2**	0
triangular prism	5	**9**	**6** ✓✓

2/2 marks

Set A Test 11

4 426 × 2 =

852 ✓ — 1/1 mark

5 Here is an algebraic expression with two variables.

$$2x + y = 8$$

List **all** the possible pairs of positive whole-number values for *x* and *y* in the table.

x	1	2	3
y	**6**	**4**	**2** ✓

1/1 mark

6 $\frac{5}{10} - \frac{2}{5} =$

$\frac{1}{10}$ ✓ — 1/1 mark

Set A Test 11

7 Sarah writes a number sequence starting at 270
She subtracts 130 each time.

Write the next two numbers in Sarah's sequence.

| 270 | 140 | 10 | **−120** | **−250** ✓ |

1/1 mark

Sarah draws a number line.

Write the missing numbers in the boxes.

−11 ... −2 ... **7** ✓ — 1/1 mark

8 Write these numbers in order, starting with the **smallest**.

0.3 $\frac{4}{5}$ $\frac{2}{10}$ 0.75

| $\frac{2}{10}$ | 0.3 | 0.75 | $\frac{4}{5}$ | ✓
smallest

1/1 mark

[END OF TEST]

Set B Answers

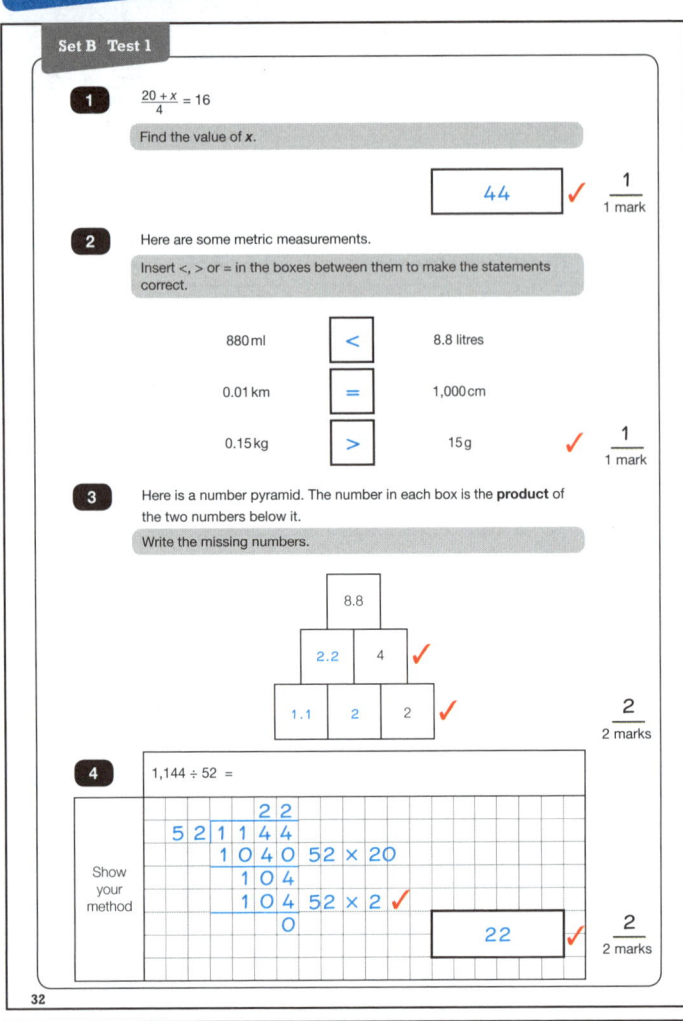

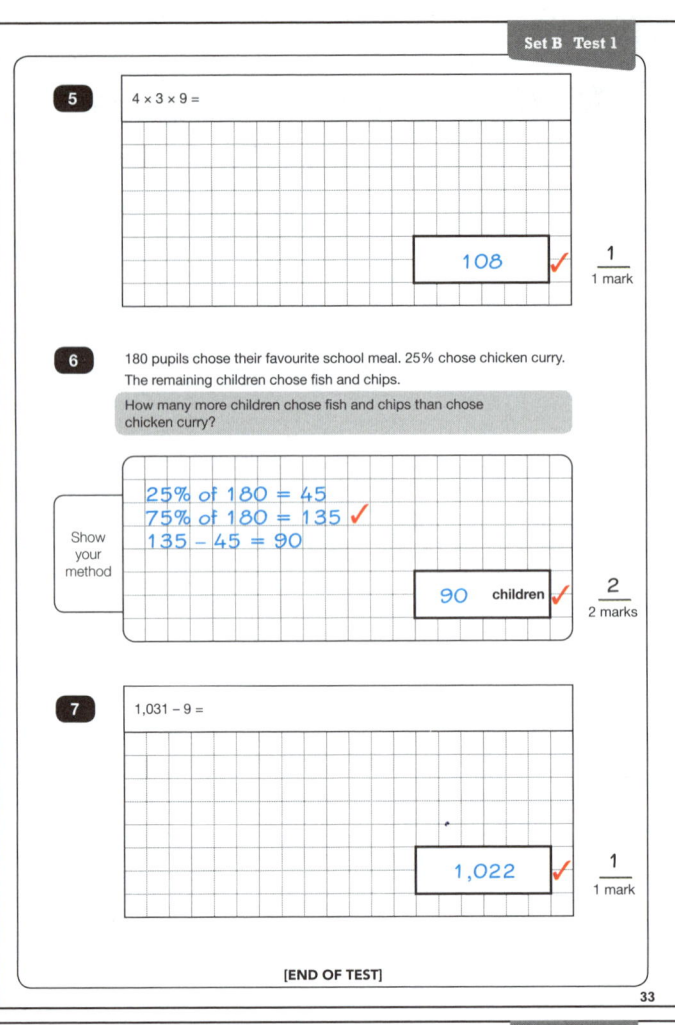

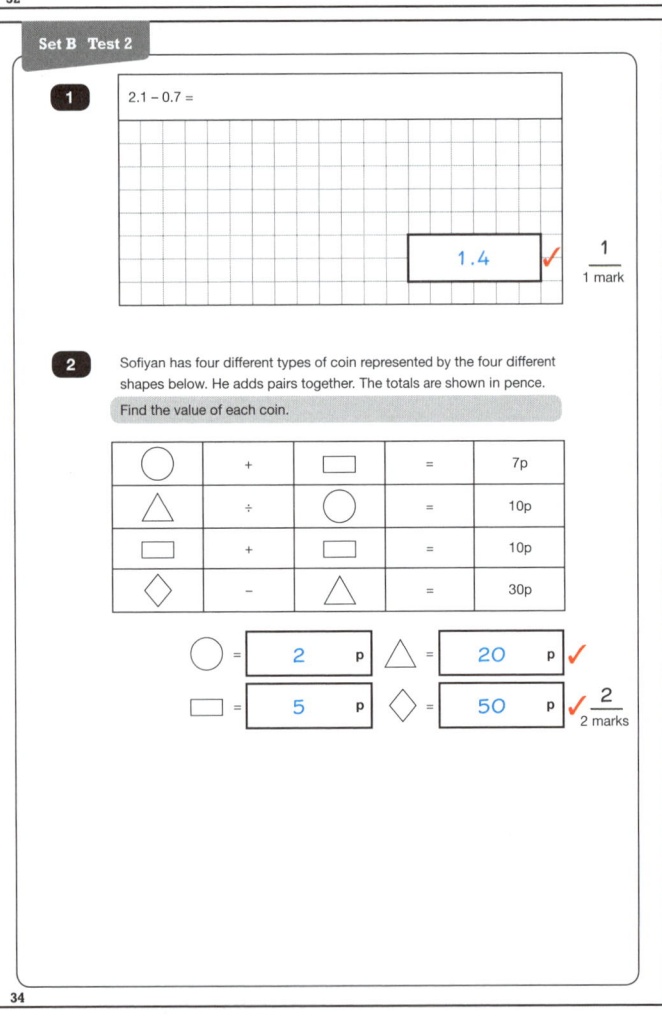

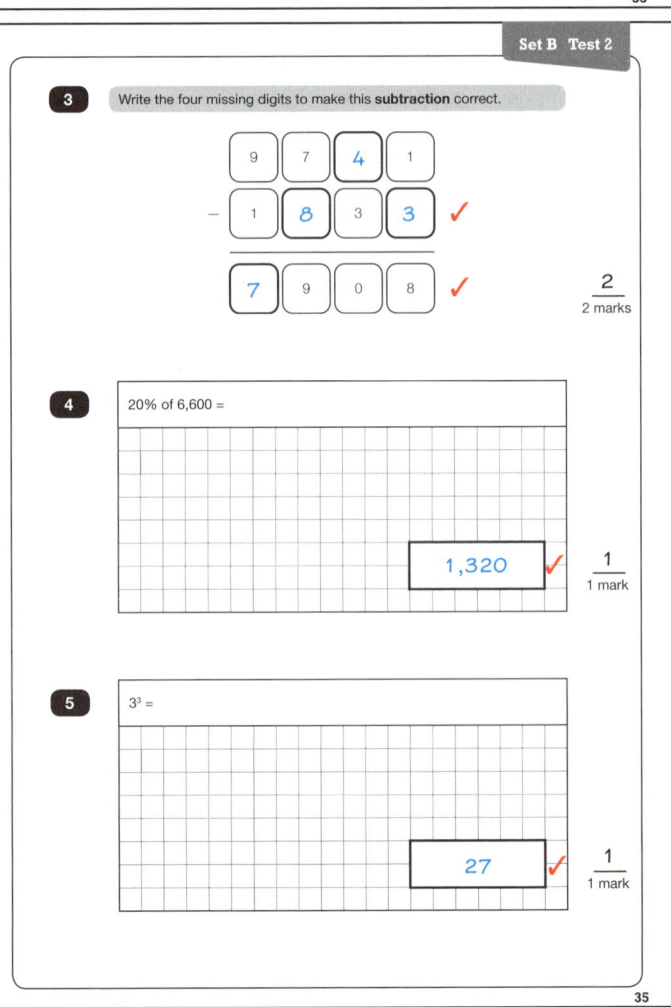

Set B Test 1

1. $\frac{20 + x}{4} = 16$

Find the value of x.

44 ✓ — 1 mark

2. Here are some metric measurements.

Insert <, > or = in the boxes between them to make the statements correct.

- 880 ml **<** 8.8 litres
- 0.01 km **=** 1,000 cm
- 0.15 kg **>** 15 g ✓

1 mark

3. Here is a number pyramid. The number in each box is the **product** of the two numbers below it.

Write the missing numbers.

```
        8.8
      2.2   4    ✓
    1.1  2   2   ✓
```

2 marks

4. $1,144 \div 52 =$

Show your method:
```
        2 2
   5 2 1 1 4 4
     1 0 4 0    52 × 20
       1 0 4
       1 0 4    52 × 2 ✓
           0
```

22 ✓ — 2 marks

5. $4 \times 3 \times 9 =$

108 ✓ — 1 mark

6. 180 pupils chose their favourite school meal. 25% chose chicken curry. The remaining children chose fish and chips.

How many more children chose fish and chips than chose chicken curry?

Show your method:
25% of 180 = 45
75% of 180 = 135 ✓
135 − 45 = 90

90 children ✓ — 2 marks

7. $1,031 - 9 =$

1,022 ✓ — 1 mark

[END OF TEST]

Set B Test 2

1. $2.1 - 0.7 =$

1.4 ✓ — 1 mark

2. Sofiyan has four different types of coin represented by the four different shapes below. He adds pairs together. The totals are shown in pence.

Find the value of each coin.

○	+	□	=	7p
△	÷	○	=	10p
□	+	□	=	10p
◇	−	△	=	30p

○ = **2** p   △ = **20** p ✓
□ = **5** p   ◇ = **50** p ✓

2 marks

3. Write the four missing digits to make this **subtraction** correct.

```
    9  7  4  1
 −  1  8  3  3   ✓
    7  9  0  8   ✓
```

2 marks

4. 20% of 6,600 =

1,320 ✓ — 1 mark

5. $3^3 =$

27 ✓ — 1 mark

Set B Answers

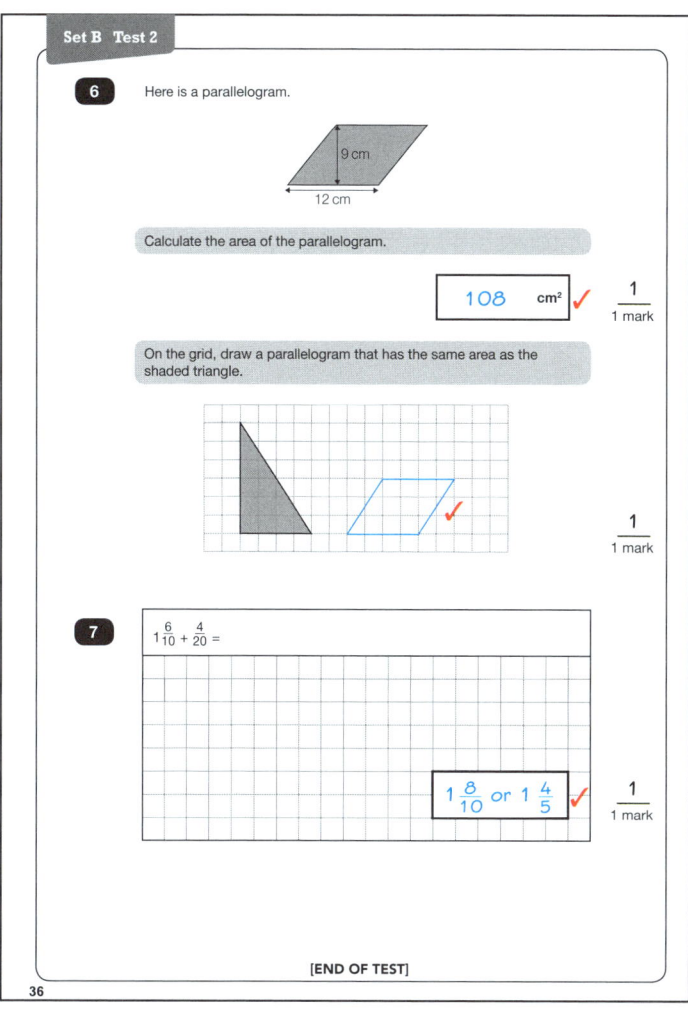

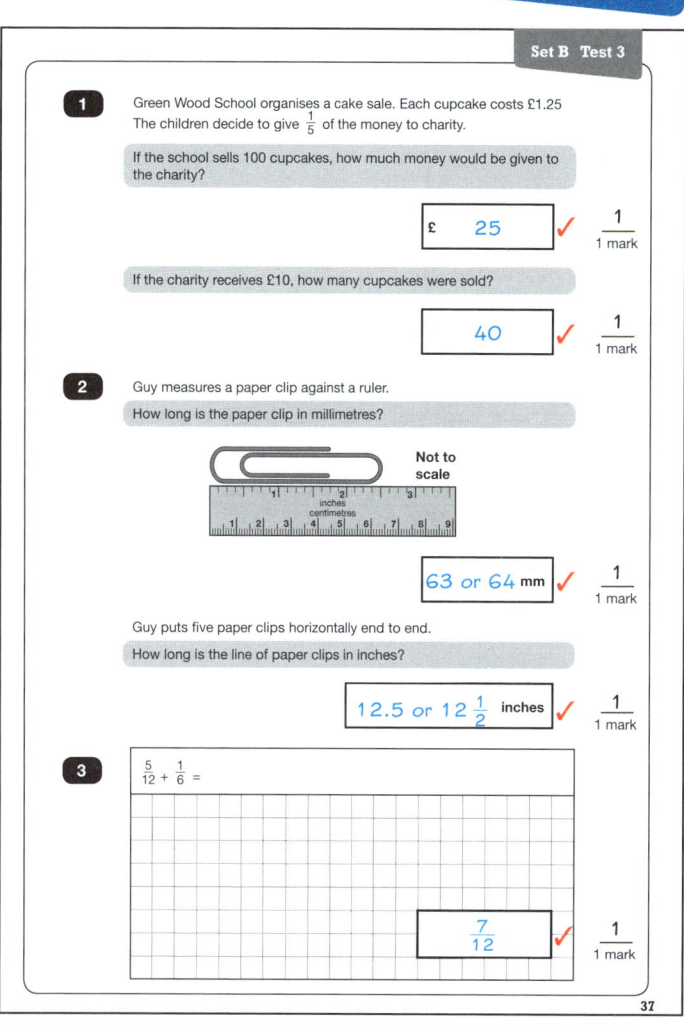

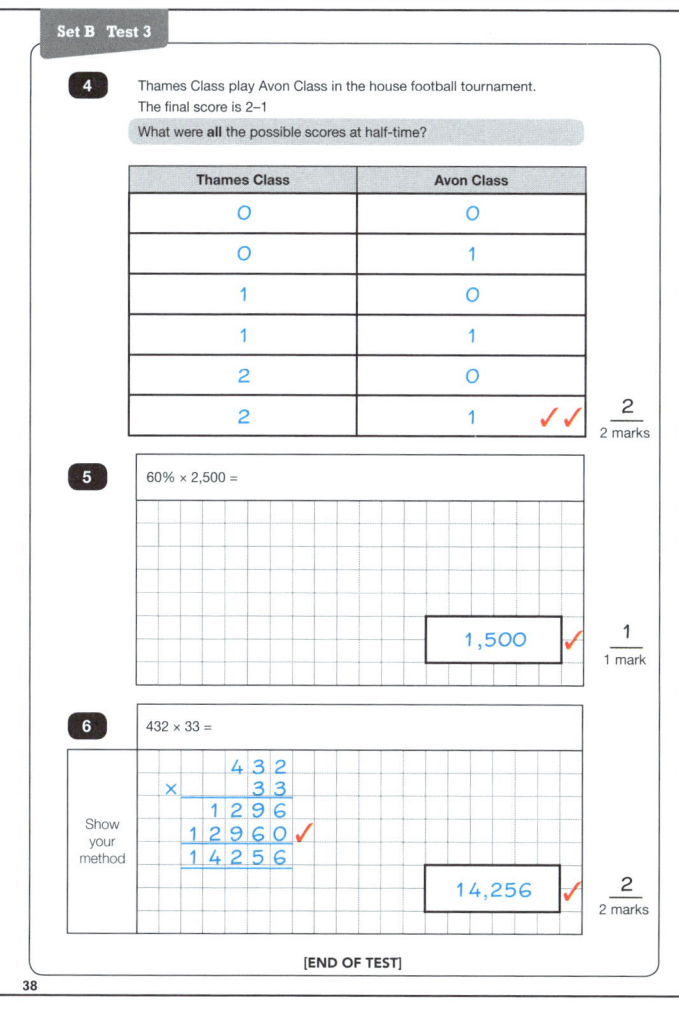

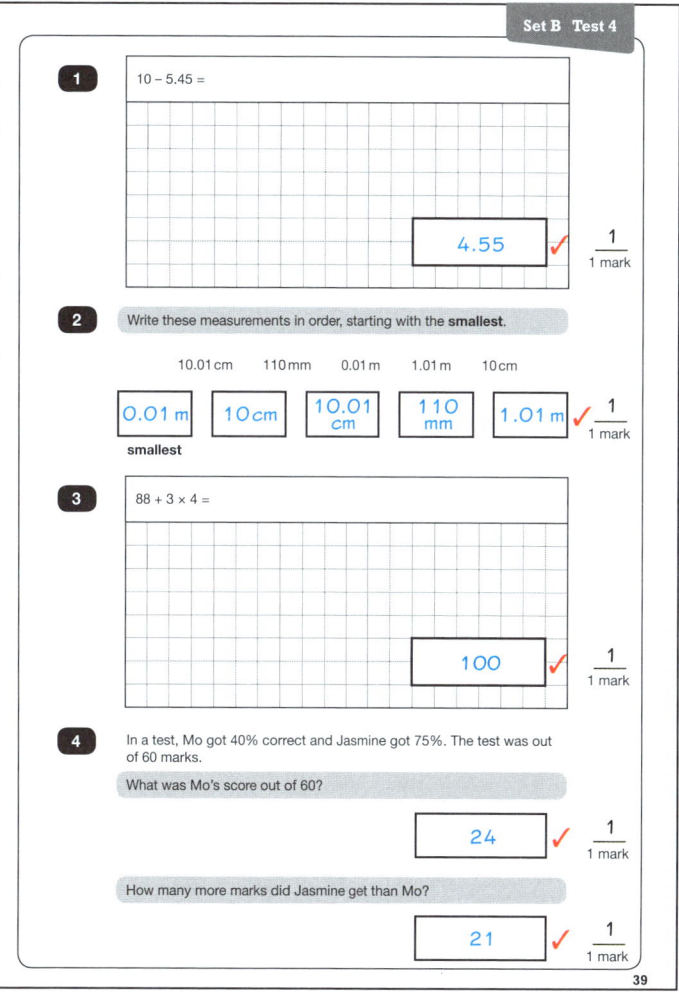

Set B Test 2

6 Here is a parallelogram.

9 cm, 12 cm

Calculate the area of the parallelogram.

108 cm² ✓ — 1/1 mark

On the grid, draw a parallelogram that has the same area as the shaded triangle.

✓ — 1/1 mark

7 $1\frac{6}{10} + \frac{4}{20} =$

$1\frac{8}{10}$ or $1\frac{4}{5}$ ✓ — 1/1 mark

[END OF TEST]

Set B Test 3

1 Green Wood School organises a cake sale. Each cupcake costs £1.25. The children decide to give $\frac{1}{5}$ of the money to charity.

If the school sells 100 cupcakes, how much money would be given to the charity?

£ **25** ✓ — 1/1 mark

If the charity receives £10, how many cupcakes were sold?

40 ✓ — 1/1 mark

2 Guy measures a paper clip against a ruler.

How long is the paper clip in millimetres?

63 or 64 mm ✓ — 1/1 mark

Guy puts five paper clips horizontally end to end.

How long is the line of paper clips in inches?

12.5 or 12½ inches ✓ — 1/1 mark

3 $\frac{5}{12} + \frac{1}{6} =$

$\frac{7}{12}$ ✓ — 1/1 mark

Set B Test 3

4 Thames Class play Avon Class in the house football tournament. The final score is 2–1.

What were **all** the possible scores at half-time?

Thames Class	Avon Class
0	0
0	1
1	0
1	1
2	0
2	1

✓✓ — 2/2 marks

5 60% × 2,500 =

1,500 ✓ — 1/1 mark

6 432 × 33 =

Show your method:
```
       4 3 2
  ×     3 3
   1 2 9 6
 1 2 9 6 0
 1 4 2 5 6
```
✓

14,256 ✓ — 2/2 marks

[END OF TEST]

Set B Test 4

1 10 − 5.45 =

4.55 ✓ — 1/1 mark

2 Write these measurements in order, starting with the **smallest**.

10.01 cm   110 mm   0.01 m   1.01 m   10 cm

0.01 m	10 cm	10.01 cm	110 mm	1.01 m
smallest				

✓ — 1/1 mark

3 88 + 3 × 4 =

100 ✓ — 1/1 mark

4 In a test, Mo got 40% correct and Jasmine got 75%. The test was out of 60 marks.

What was Mo's score out of 60?

24 ✓ — 1/1 mark

How many more marks did Jasmine get than Mo?

21 ✓ — 1/1 mark

Set B Answers

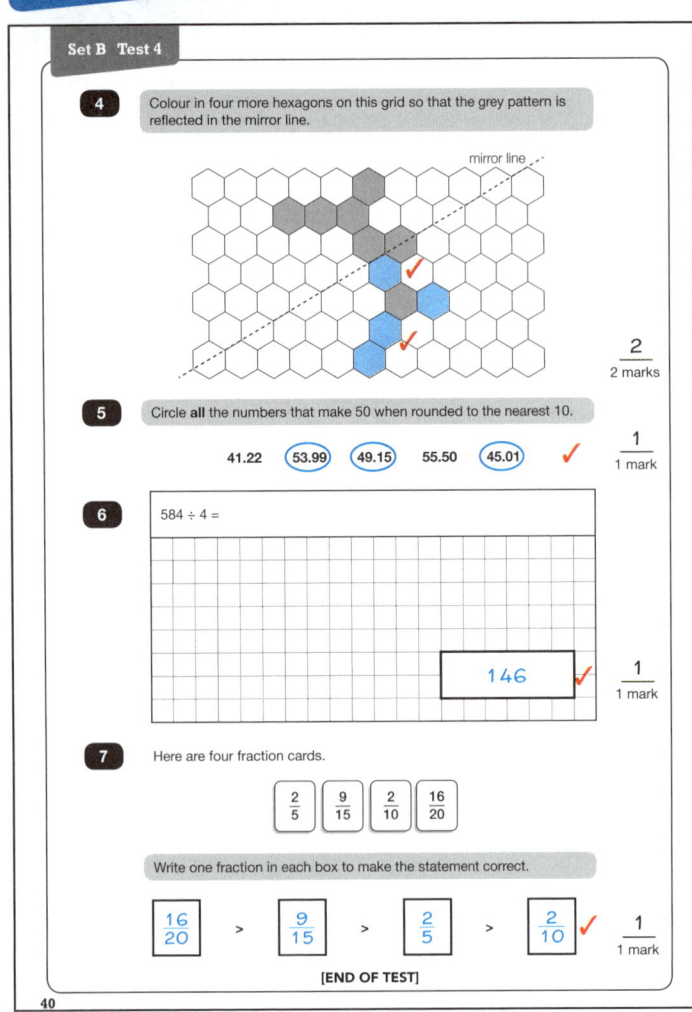

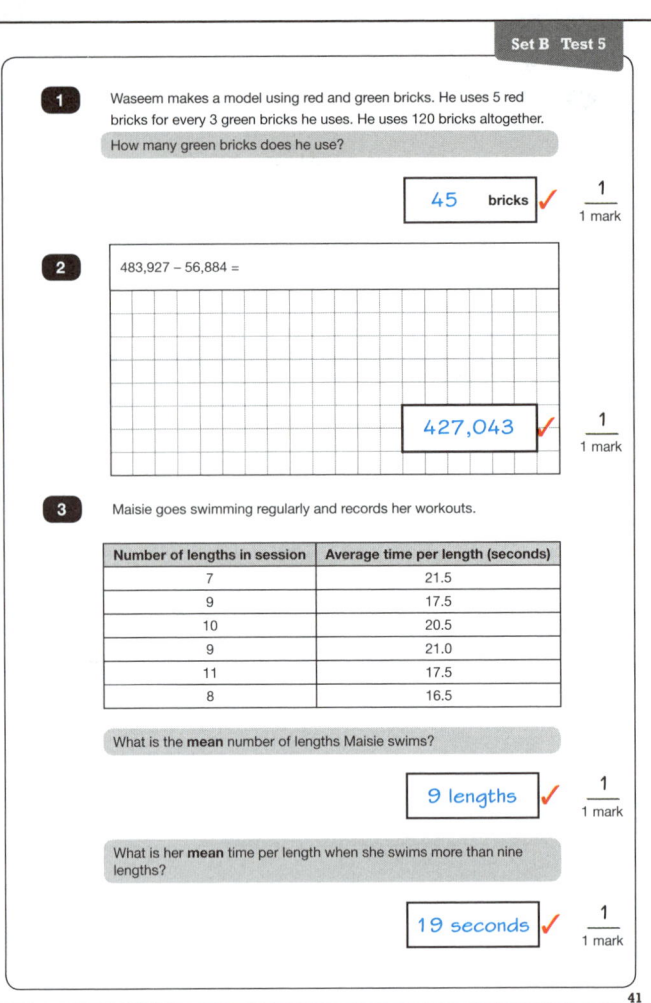

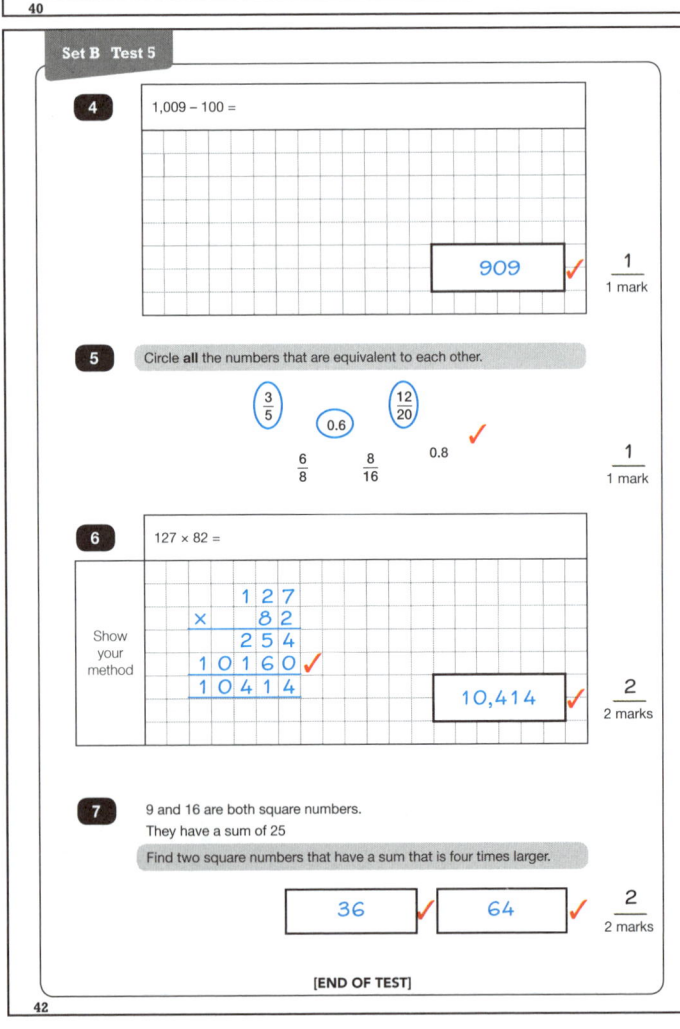

Set B Test 4

4 Colour in four more hexagons on this grid so that the grey pattern is reflected in the mirror line.

2 / 2 marks

5 Circle **all** the numbers that make 50 when rounded to the nearest 10.

41.22   (53.99)   (49.15)   55.50   (45.01)

1 / 1 mark

6 584 ÷ 4 =

146

1 / 1 mark

7 Here are four fraction cards.

$\frac{2}{5}$ $\frac{9}{15}$ $\frac{2}{10}$ $\frac{16}{20}$

Write one fraction in each box to make the statement correct.

$\frac{16}{20}$ > $\frac{9}{15}$ > $\frac{2}{5}$ > $\frac{2}{10}$

1 / 1 mark

[END OF TEST]

Set B Test 5

1 Waseem makes a model using red and green bricks. He uses 5 red bricks for every 3 green bricks he uses. He uses 120 bricks altogether.

How many green bricks does he use?

45 bricks

1 / 1 mark

2 483,927 − 56,884 =

427,043

1 / 1 mark

3 Maisie goes swimming regularly and records her workouts.

Number of lengths in session	Average time per length (seconds)
7	21.5
9	17.5
10	20.5
9	21.0
11	17.5
8	16.5

What is the **mean** number of lengths Maisie swims?

9 lengths

1 / 1 mark

What is her **mean** time per length when she swims more than nine lengths?

19 seconds

1 / 1 mark

Set B Test 5

4 1,009 − 100 =

909

1 / 1 mark

5 Circle **all** the numbers that are equivalent to each other.

$(\frac{3}{5})$ $(\frac{12}{20})$ (0.6) $\frac{6}{8}$ $\frac{8}{16}$ 0.8

1 / 1 mark

6 127 × 82 =

Show your method:
```
    1 2 7
  ×   8 2
    2 5 4
  1 0 1 6 0
  1 0 4 1 4
```

10,414

2 / 2 marks

7 9 and 16 are both square numbers. They have a sum of 25.

Find two square numbers that have a sum that is four times larger.

36   **64**

2 / 2 marks

[END OF TEST]

Set B Test 6

1 983 + 100 =

1,083

1 / 1 mark

2 Annie draws the nets for two cuboids, A and B, on centimetre-squared paper.

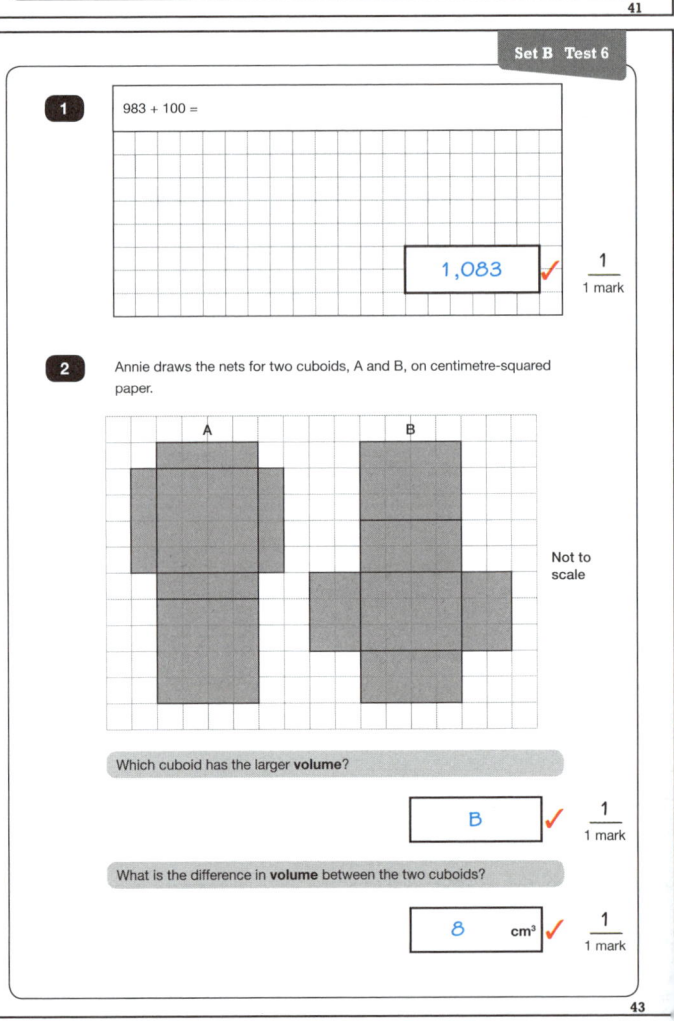

Not to scale

Which cuboid has the larger **volume**?

B

1 / 1 mark

What is the difference in **volume** between the two cuboids?

8 cm³

1 / 1 mark

Set B Answers

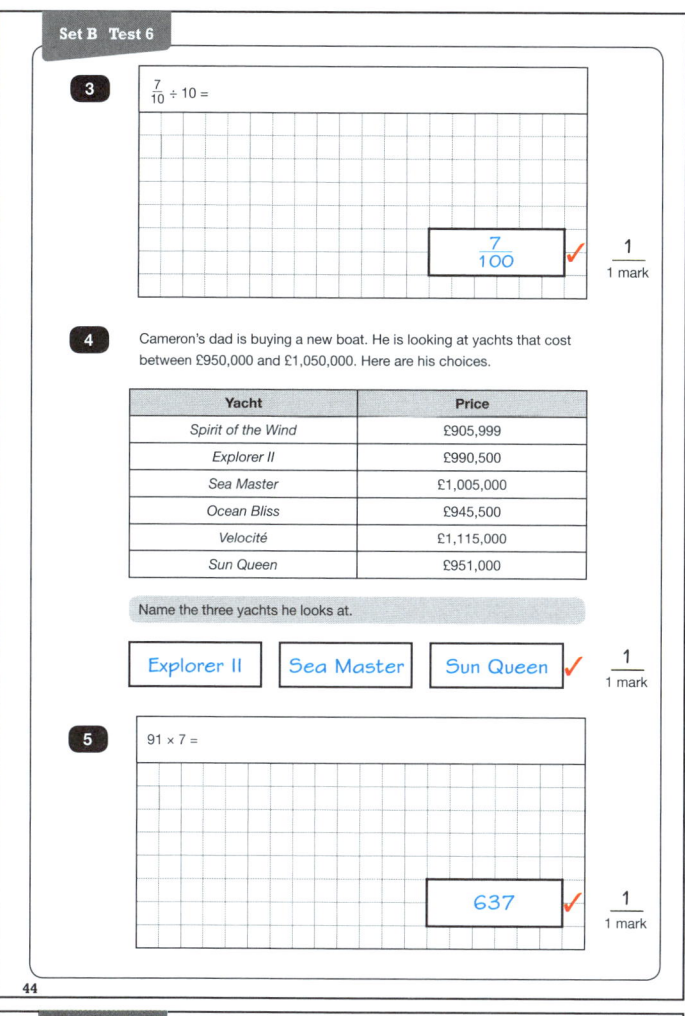

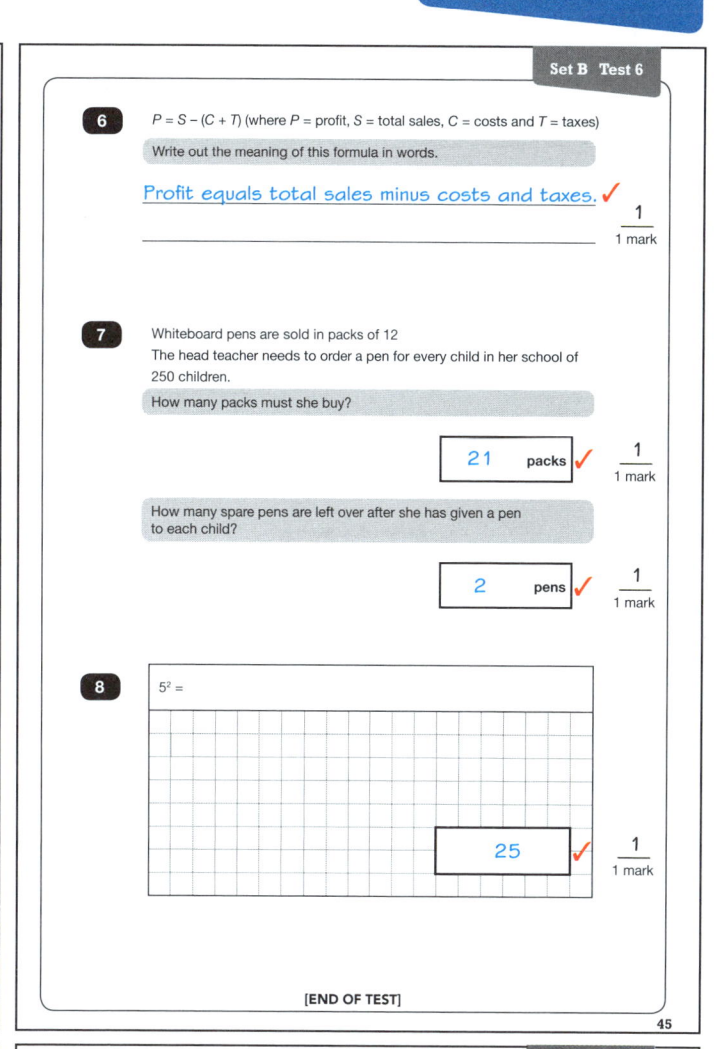

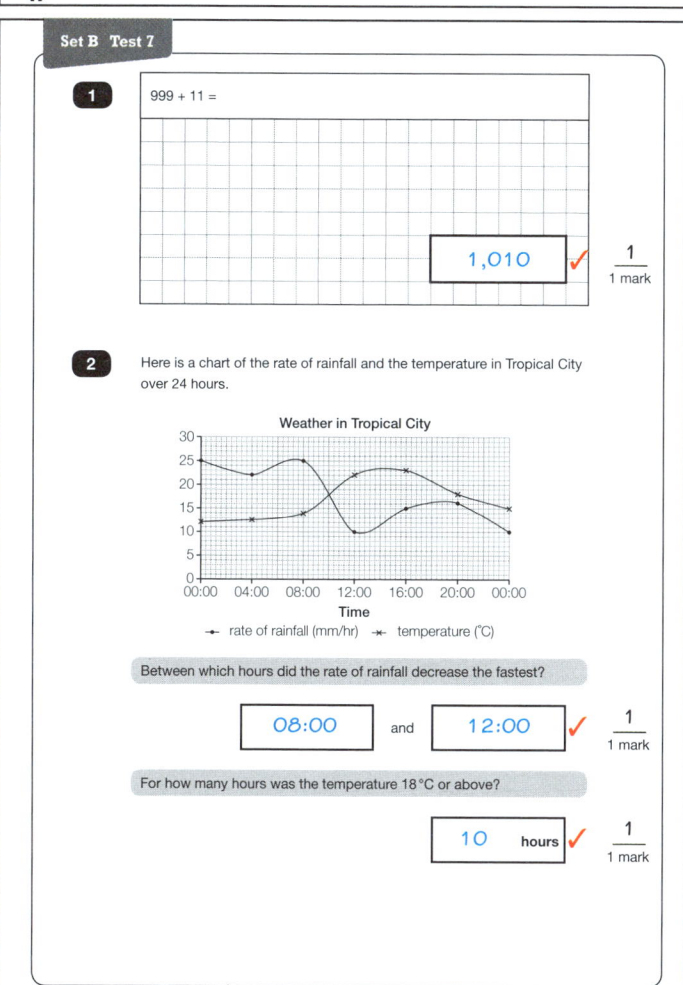

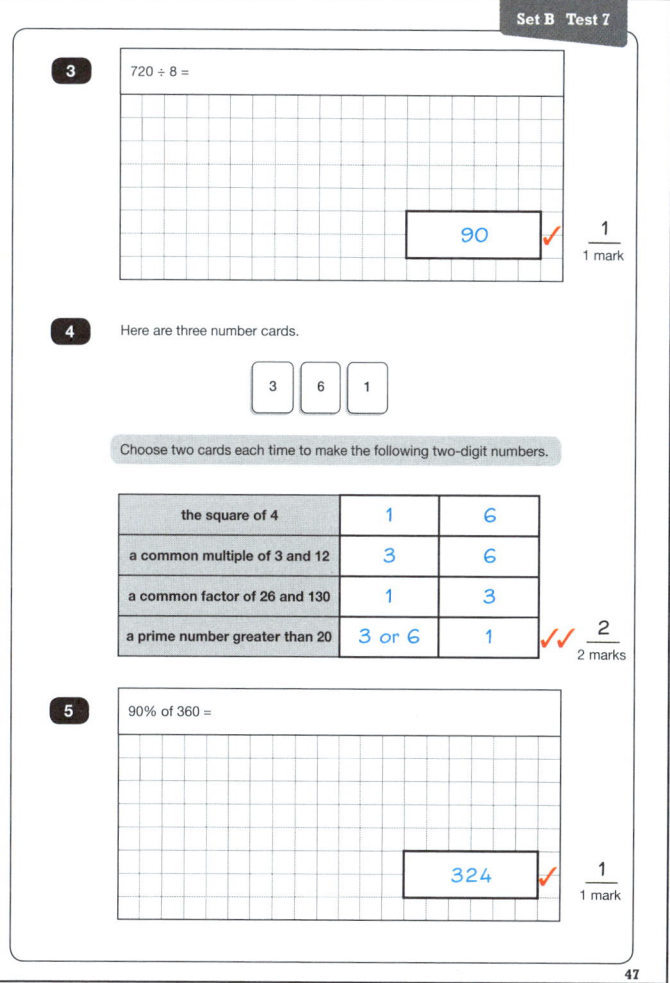

Set B Test 6

3 $\frac{7}{10} \div 10 =$

$\frac{7}{100}$ ✓ — 1 / 1 mark

4 Cameron's dad is buying a new boat. He is looking at yachts that cost between £950,000 and £1,050,000. Here are his choices.

Yacht	Price
Spirit of the Wind	£905,999
Explorer II	£990,500
Sea Master	£1,005,000
Ocean Bliss	£945,500
Velocité	£1,115,000
Sun Queen	£951,000

Name the three yachts he looks at.

Explorer II   Sea Master   Sun Queen ✓ — 1 / 1 mark

5 91 × 7 =

637 ✓ — 1 / 1 mark

6 $P = S - (C + T)$ (where P = profit, S = total sales, C = costs and T = taxes)

Write out the meaning of this formula in words.

Profit equals total sales minus costs and taxes. ✓ — 1 / 1 mark

7 Whiteboard pens are sold in packs of 12
The head teacher needs to order a pen for every child in her school of 250 children.

How many packs must she buy?

21 packs ✓ — 1 / 1 mark

How many spare pens are left over after she has given a pen to each child?

2 pens ✓ — 1 / 1 mark

8 $5^2 =$

25 ✓ — 1 / 1 mark

[END OF TEST]

Set B Test 7

1 999 + 11 =

1,010 ✓ — 1 / 1 mark

2 Here is a chart of the rate of rainfall and the temperature in Tropical City over 24 hours.

Weather in Tropical City (chart with rate of rainfall (mm/hr) and temperature (°C) over Time 00:00–00:00)

Between which hours did the rate of rainfall decrease the fastest?

08:00 and 12:00 ✓ — 1 / 1 mark

For how many hours was the temperature 18 °C or above?

10 hours ✓ — 1 / 1 mark

3 720 ÷ 8 =

90 ✓ — 1 / 1 mark

4 Here are three number cards.

3   6   1

Choose two cards each time to make the following two-digit numbers.

the square of 4	1	6
a common multiple of 3 and 12	3	6
a common factor of 26 and 130	1	3
a prime number greater than 20	3 or 6	1

✓✓ — 2 / 2 marks

5 90% of 360 =

324 ✓ — 1 / 1 mark

Set B Answers

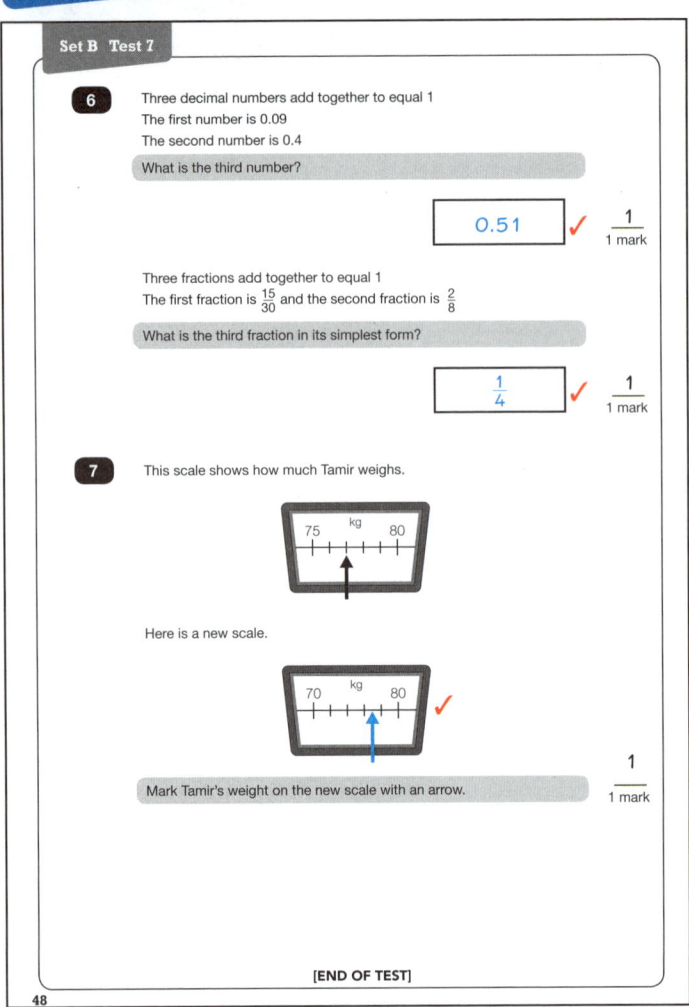

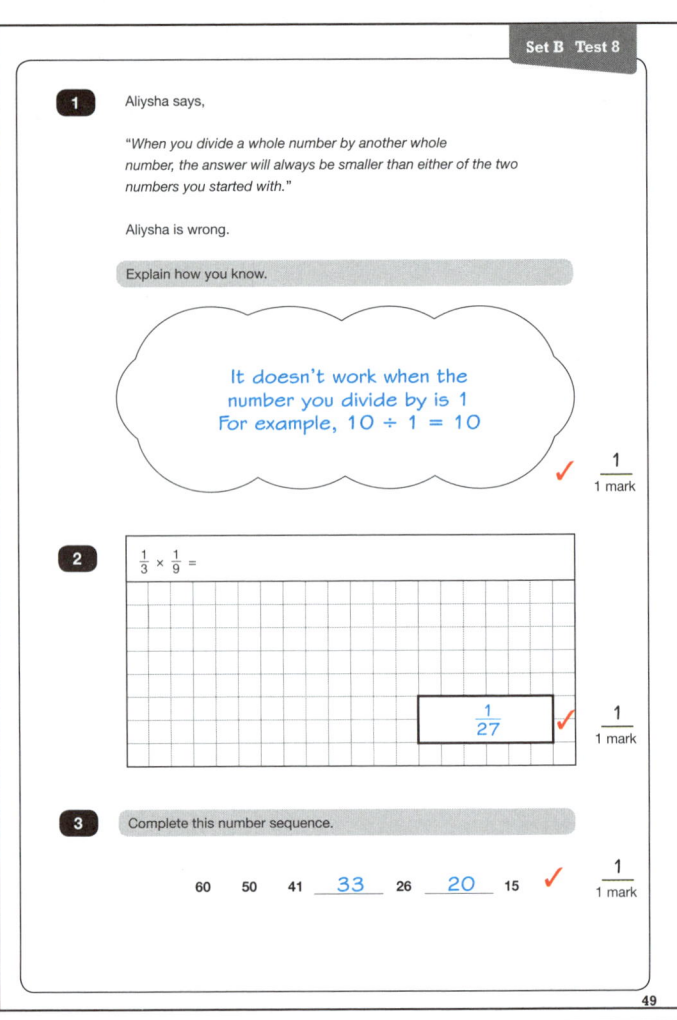

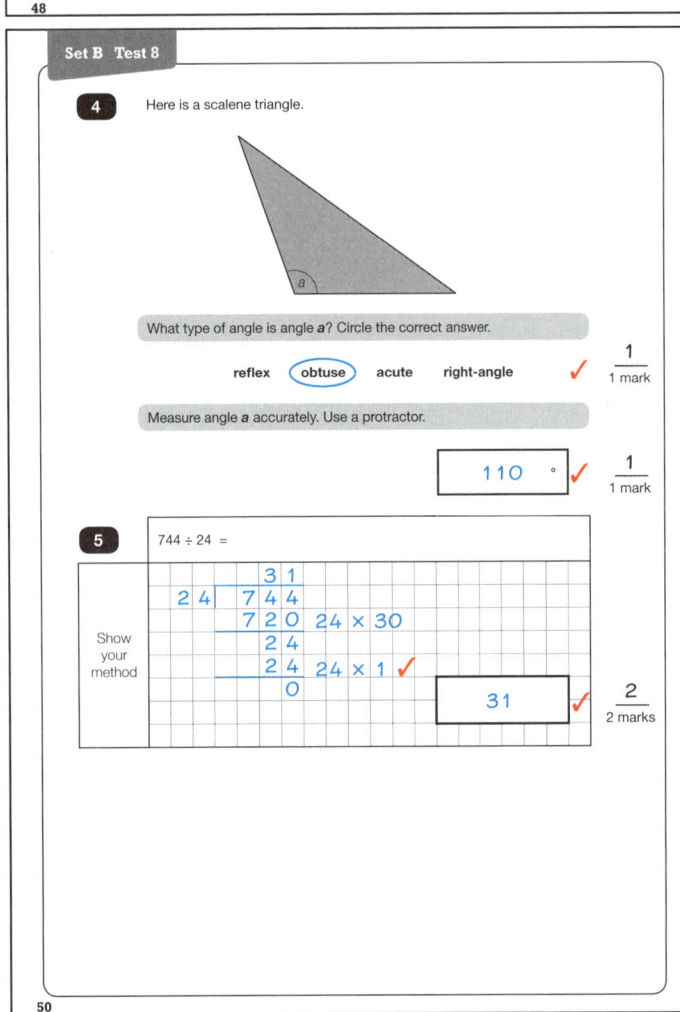

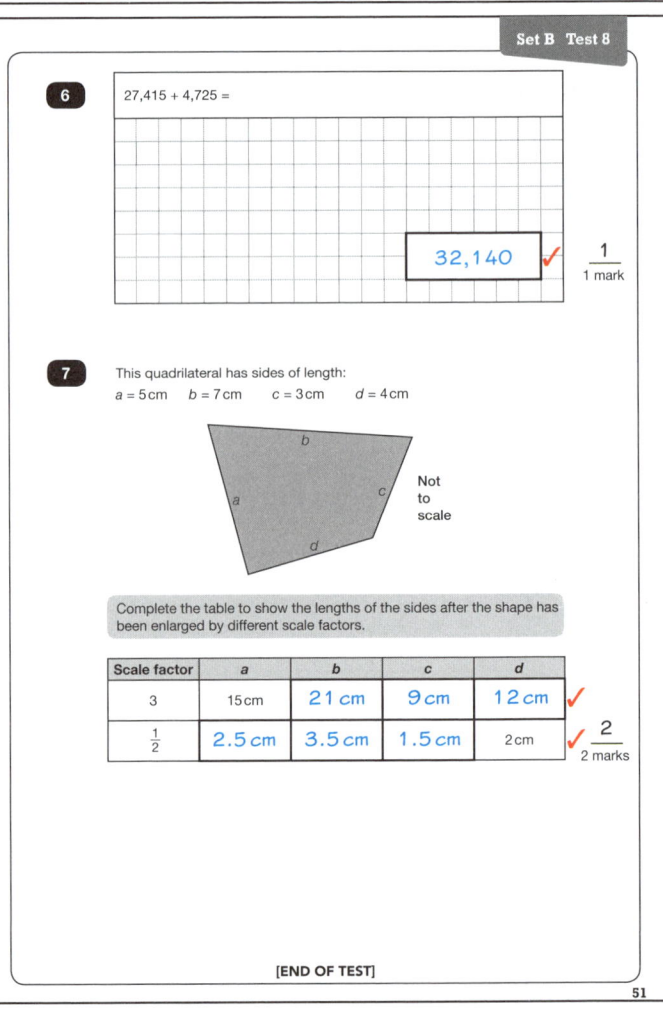

Set B Test 7

6 Three decimal numbers add together to equal 1
The first number is 0.09
The second number is 0.4
What is the third number?

0.51 ✓ 1/1 mark

Three fractions add together to equal 1
The first fraction is $\frac{15}{30}$ and the second fraction is $\frac{2}{8}$
What is the third fraction in its simplest form?

$\frac{1}{4}$ ✓ 1/1 mark

7 This scale shows how much Tamir weighs.

Here is a new scale.

Mark Tamir's weight on the new scale with an arrow. ✓ 1/1 mark

[END OF TEST]

Set B Test 8

1 Aliysha says,

"When you divide a whole number by another whole number, the answer will always be smaller than either of the two numbers you started with."

Aliysha is wrong.

Explain how you know.

It doesn't work when the number you divide by is 1. For example, 10 ÷ 1 = 10 ✓ 1/1 mark

2 $\frac{1}{3} \times \frac{1}{9} =$

$\frac{1}{27}$ ✓ 1/1 mark

3 Complete this number sequence.

60   50   41   **33**   26   **20**   15 ✓ 1/1 mark

Set B Test 8

4 Here is a scalene triangle.

What type of angle is angle *a*? Circle the correct answer.

reflex   (**obtuse**)   acute   right-angle ✓ 1/1 mark

Measure angle *a* accurately. Use a protractor.

110 ° ✓ 1/1 mark

5 744 ÷ 24 =

Show your method:
```
     3 1
24) 7 4 4
    7 2 0   24 × 30
    ─────
      2 4
      2 4   24 × 1 ✓
    ─────
        0
```

31 ✓ 2/2 marks

6 27,415 + 4,725 =

32,140 ✓ 1/1 mark

7 This quadrilateral has sides of length:
a = 5 cm   *b* = 7 cm   *c* = 3 cm   *d* = 4 cm

Not to scale

Complete the table to show the lengths of the sides after the shape has been enlarged by different scale factors.

Scale factor	a	b	c	d
3	15 cm	21 cm	9 cm	12 cm
$\frac{1}{2}$	2.5 cm	3.5 cm	1.5 cm	2 cm

✓ 2/2 marks

[END OF TEST]

Set B Answers

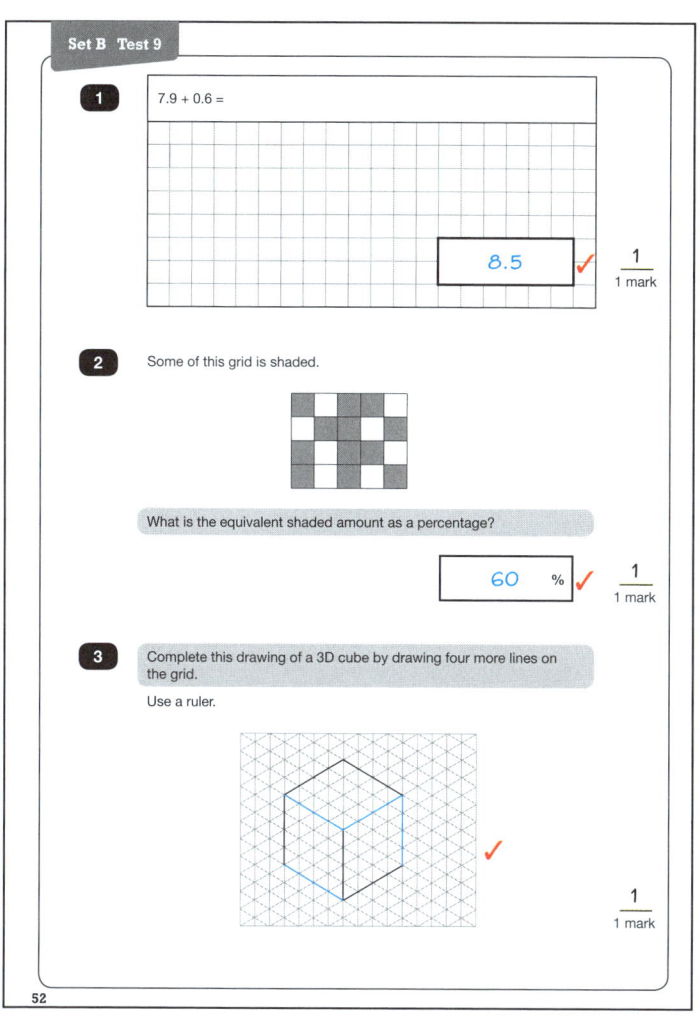

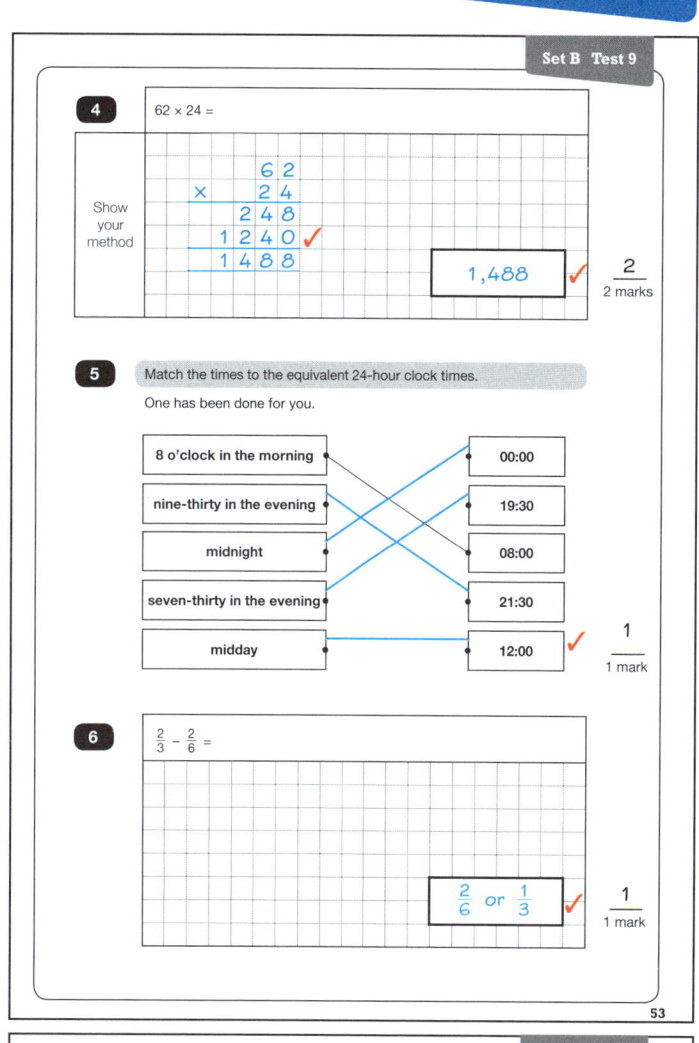

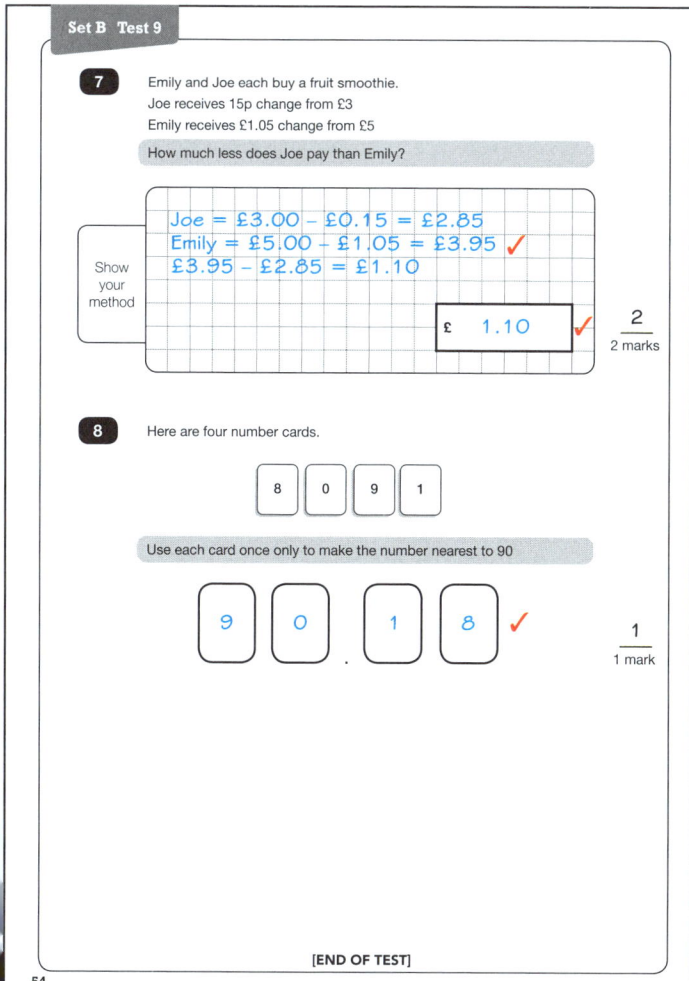

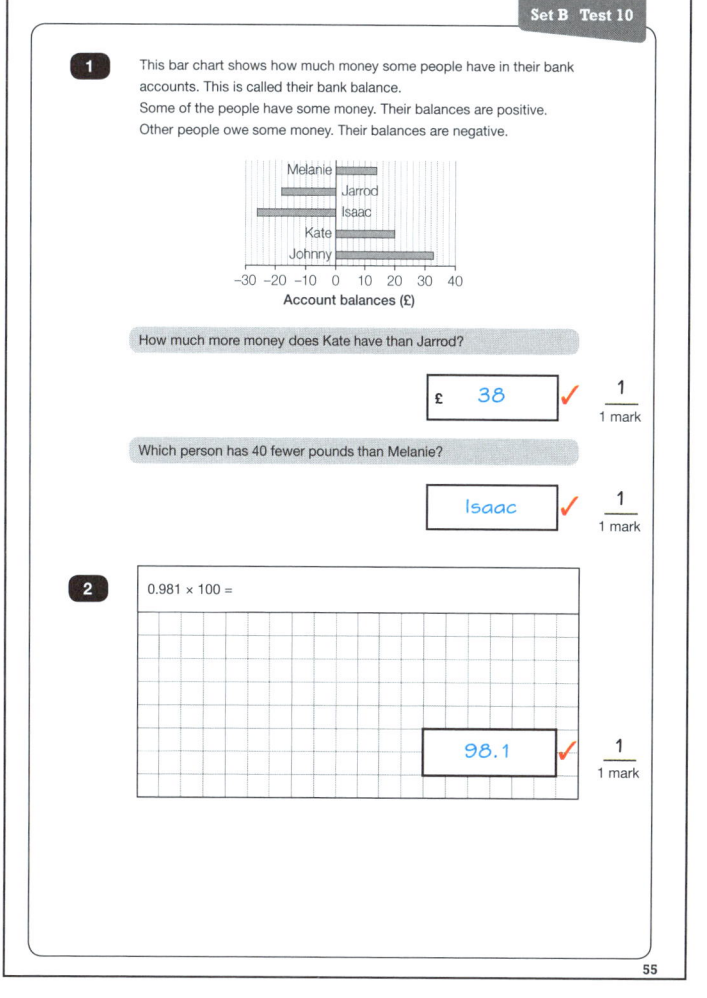

Set B Test 9

1 $7.9 + 0.6 =$

8.5 ✓ — 1 mark

2 Some of this grid is shaded.

What is the equivalent shaded amount as a percentage?

60 % ✓ — 1 mark

3 Complete this drawing of a 3D cube by drawing four more lines on the grid.

Use a ruler.

✓ — 1 mark

4 $62 \times 24 =$

Show your method:
```
     6 2
  ×  2 4
   2 4 8
 1 2 4 0  ✓
 1 4 8 8
```
1,488 ✓ — 2 marks

5 Match the times to the equivalent 24-hour clock times.
One has been done for you.

- 8 o'clock in the morning → 08:00
- nine-thirty in the evening → 21:30
- midnight → 00:00
- seven-thirty in the evening → 19:30
- midday → 12:00 ✓

1 mark

6 $\frac{2}{3} - \frac{2}{6} =$

$\frac{2}{6}$ or $\frac{1}{3}$ ✓ — 1 mark

7 Emily and Joe each buy a fruit smoothie.
Joe receives 15p change from £3
Emily receives £1.05 change from £5

How much less does Joe pay than Emily?

Show your method:
Joe = £3.00 − £0.15 = £2.85
Emily = £5.00 − £1.05 = £3.95 ✓
£3.95 − £2.85 = £1.10

£ 1.10 ✓ — 2 marks

8 Here are four number cards.

8 0 9 1

Use each card once only to make the number nearest to 90

9 0 . 1 8 ✓ — 1 mark

[END OF TEST]

Set B Test 10

1 This bar chart shows how much money some people have in their bank accounts. This is called their bank balance.
Some of the people have some money. Their balances are positive.
Other people owe some money. Their balances are negative.

How much more money does Kate have than Jarrod?

£ 38 ✓ — 1 mark

Which person has 40 fewer pounds than Melanie?

Isaac ✓ — 1 mark

2 $0.981 \times 100 =$

98.1 ✓ — 1 mark

Set B Answers

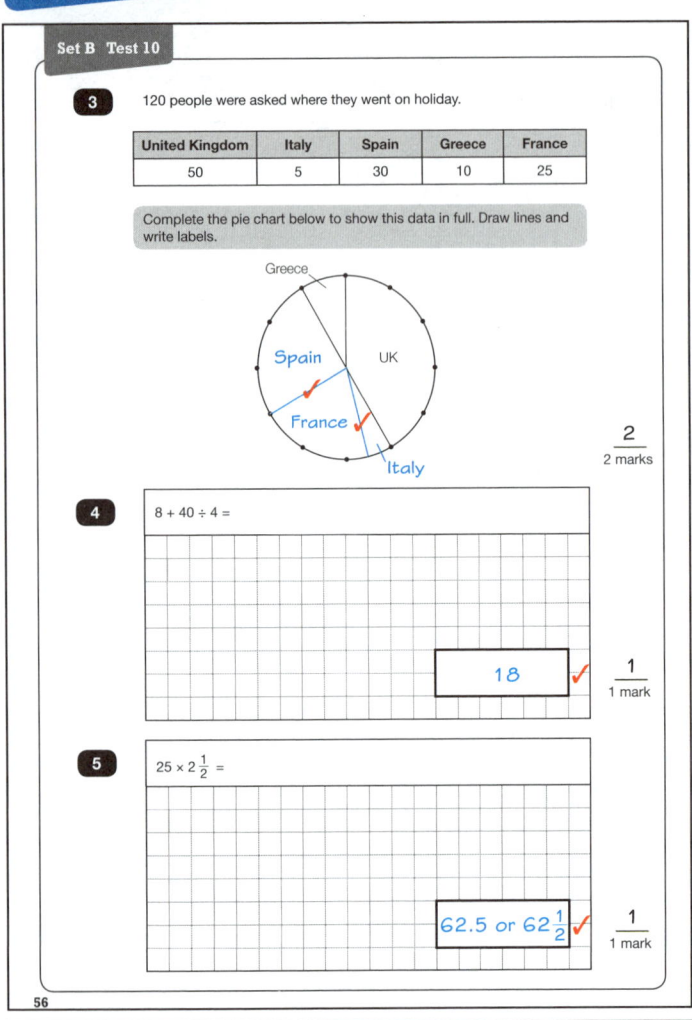

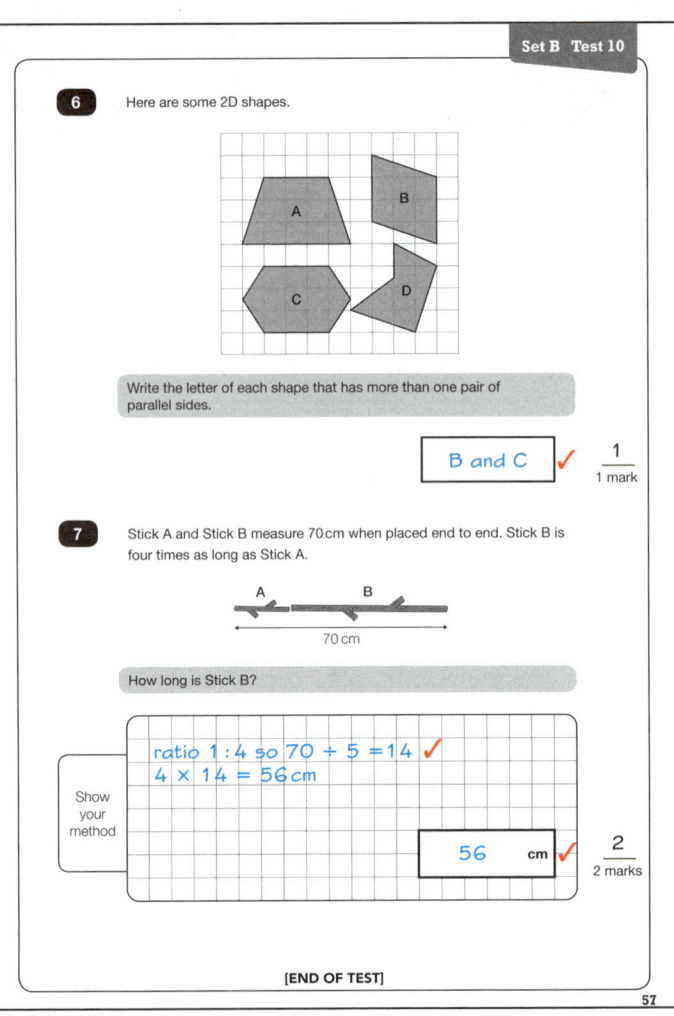

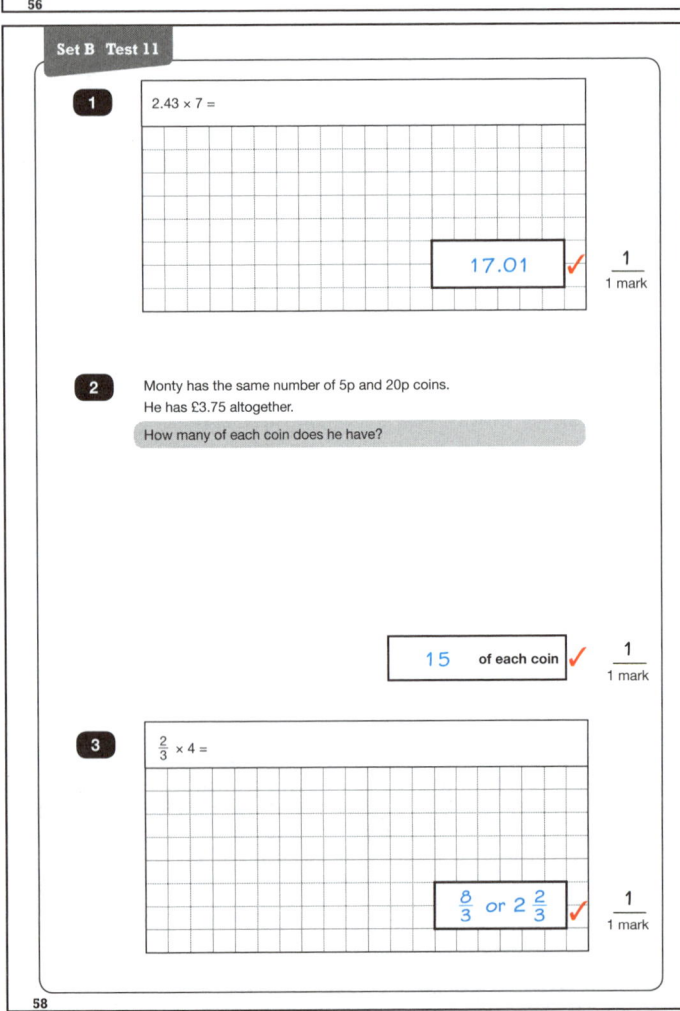

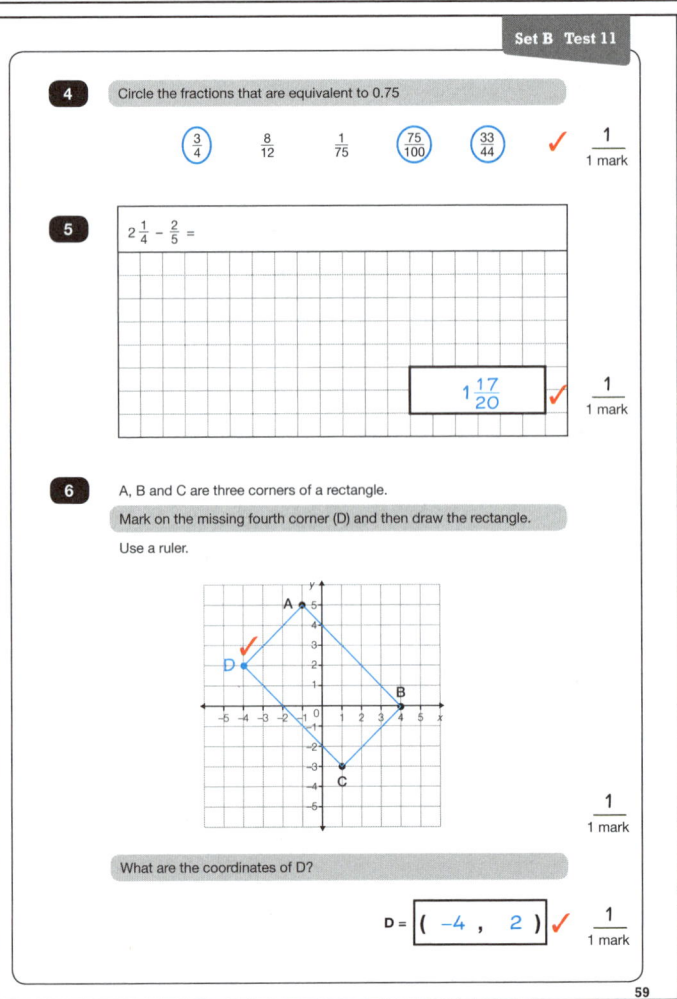

Set B Test 10

3 120 people were asked where they went on holiday.

United Kingdom	Italy	Spain	Greece	France
50	5	30	10	25

Complete the pie chart below to show this data in full. Draw lines and write labels.

Pie chart labelled: Greece, Spain, UK, France, Italy ✓

2 / 2 marks

4 $8 + 40 \div 4 =$

18 ✓ **1 / 1 mark**

5 $25 \times 2\frac{1}{2} =$

62.5 or $62\frac{1}{2}$ ✓ **1 / 1 mark**

Set B Test 10

6 Here are some 2D shapes.

Write the letter of each shape that has more than one pair of parallel sides.

B and C ✓ **1 / 1 mark**

7 Stick A and Stick B measure 70 cm when placed end to end. Stick B is four times as long as Stick A.

How long is Stick B?

Show your method:
ratio 1 : 4 so 70 ÷ 5 = 14 ✓
4 × 14 = 56 cm

56 cm ✓ **2 / 2 marks**

[END OF TEST]

Set B Test 11

1 $2.43 \times 7 =$

17.01 ✓ **1 / 1 mark**

2 Monty has the same number of 5p and 20p coins.
He has £3.75 altogether.
How many of each coin does he have?

15 of each coin ✓ **1 / 1 mark**

3 $\frac{2}{3} \times 4 =$

$\frac{8}{3}$ or $2\frac{2}{3}$ ✓ **1 / 1 mark**

Set B Test 11

4 Circle the fractions that are equivalent to 0.75

$\boxed{\frac{3}{4}}$ $\frac{8}{12}$ $\frac{1}{75}$ $\boxed{\frac{75}{100}}$ $\boxed{\frac{33}{44}}$ ✓ **1 / 1 mark**

5 $2\frac{1}{4} - \frac{2}{5} =$

$1\frac{17}{20}$ ✓ **1 / 1 mark**

6 A, B and C are three corners of a rectangle.
Mark on the missing fourth corner (D) and then draw the rectangle.
Use a ruler.

✓ **1 / 1 mark**

What are the coordinates of D?

D = (−4 , 2) ✓ **1 / 1 mark**

Set B Test 11

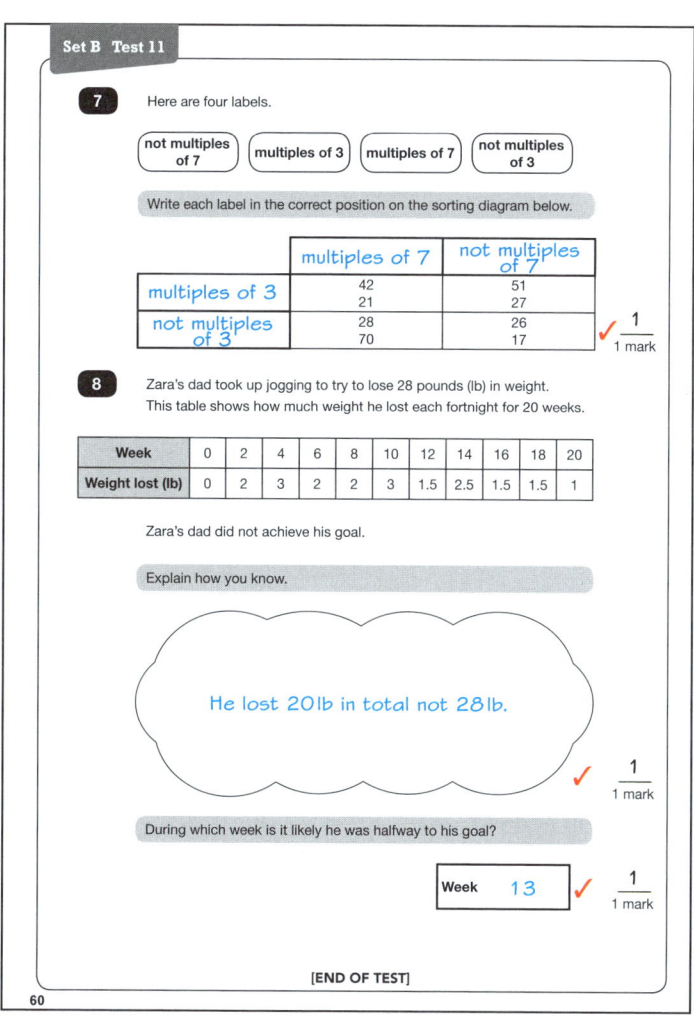

7 Here are four labels.

> not multiples of 7 | multiples of 3 | multiples of 7 | not multiples of 3

Write each label in the correct position on the sorting diagram below.

	multiples of 7	not multiples of 7
multiples of 3	42 21	51 27
not multiples of 3	28 70	26 17

✓ 1 / 1 mark

8 Zara's dad took up jogging to try to lose 28 pounds (lb) in weight.
This table shows how much weight he lost each fortnight for 20 weeks.

Week	0	2	4	6	8	10	12	14	16	18	20
Weight lost (lb)	0	2	3	2	2	3	1.5	2.5	1.5	1.5	1

Zara's dad did not achieve his goal.

Explain how you know.

> He lost 20lb in total not 28lb.

✓ 1 / 1 mark

During which week is it likely he was halfway to his goal?

Week **13**   ✓ 1 / 1 mark

[END OF TEST]

Published by Pearson Education Limited, 80 Strand, London, WC2R 0RL.

www.pearsonschools.co.uk

Text © Pearson Education Limited 2017
Edited, typeset and produced by Elektra Media Ltd
Original illustrations © Pearson Education Limited 2017
Illustrated by Elektra Media Ltd
Cover illustration by Ana Albero

The right of Giles Clare to be identified as author of this work has been asserted by him in accordance with the Copyright, Designs and Patents Act 1988.

First published 2017

20 19 18 17
10 9 8 7 6 5 4 3 2 1

British Library Cataloguing in Publication Data
A catalogue record for this book is available from the British Library.

ISBN 978 1 292 21667 6

Copyright notice
All rights reserved. No part of this publication may be reproduced in any form or by any means (including photocopying or storing it in any medium by electronic means and whether or not transiently or incidentally to some other use of this publication) without the written permission of the copyright owner, except in accordance with the provisions of the Copyright, Designs and Patents Act 1988 or under the terms of a licence issued by the Copyright Licensing Agency, Barnard's Inn, 86 Fetter Lane, London, EC4A 1EN (www.cla.co.uk). Applications for the copyright owner's written permission should be addressed to the publisher.

Printed in Slovakia by Neografia

Acknowledgements
Contains public sector information licensed under the Open Government Licence v3.0

Note from publisher
Pearson has robust editorial processes, including answer and fact checks, to ensure the accuracy of the content in this publication, and every effort is made to ensure this publication is free of errors. We are, however, only human, and occasionally errors do occur. Pearson is not liable for any misunderstandings that arise as a result of errors in this publication, but it is our priority to ensure that the content is accurate. If you spot an error, please do contact us at resourcescorrections@pearson.com so we can make sure it is corrected.